# INCREASING THE COMPETITIVE EDGE IN MATH AND SCIENCE

### Edited by
### Janet S. Kettlewell and
### Ronald J. Henry

ROWMAN & LITTLEFIELD EDUCATION
Lanham • New York • Toronto • Plymouth, UK

Published in the United States of America
by Rowman & Littlefield Education
A Division of Rowman & Littlefield Publishers, Inc.
A wholly owned subsidiary of The Rowman & Littlefield Publishing Group, Inc.
4501 Forbes Boulevard, Suite 200, Lanham, Maryland 20706
www.rowmaneducation.com

Estover Road
Plymouth PL6 7PY
United Kingdom

Copyright © 2009 by Janet S. Kettlewell and Ronald J. Henry

British Library Cataloguing in Publication Information Available

**Library of Congress Cataloging-in-Publication Data**

Kettlewell, Janet S., 1943-
  Increasing the competitive edge in math and science / Janet S. Kettlewell and Ronald
J. Henry.
     p. cm.
  Includes bibliographical references.
  ISBN 978-1-60709-013-7 (cloth : alk. paper) — ISBN 978-1-60709-014-4 (pbk. : alk.
paper) — ISBN 978-1-60709-015-1 (ebook)
  1. Mathematics—Study and teaching—United States. 2. Science—Study and
teaching—United States. 3. Education and state—United States. 4. Academic
achievement—United States. I. Henry, Ronald J. II. Title.
  QA13.K48 2009
  510.71'073—dc22                                                        2008049345

∞™ The paper used in this publication meets the minimum requirements of
American National Standard for Information Sciences—Permanence of
Paper for Printed Library Materials, ANSI/NISO Z39.48-1992.
Manufactured in the United States of America.

# CONTENTS

# ACKNOWLEDGMENTS

The editors wish to acknowledge the significant work of the authors of the ten chapters included in *Increasing the Competitive Edge in Math and Science*. In addition, the editors wish to acknowledge the contributions of the individuals listed below for their ideas, feedback, and/or technical assistance in the preparation of this manuscript.

Juan-Carlos Aguilar, science program manager, Georgia Department of Education

Amanda Buice, program specialist, Math Science Partnership, Georgia Department of Education

Sara Connor (retired), senior executive director, P–16 Special Initiatives and Operations, University System of Georgia

Janet Davis, mathematics education specialist on academic standards, Georgia Department of Education

Michael Lariscy, College of Education coordinator for Armstrong Atlantic State University, Partnership for Reform In Science and Mathematics (PRISM)

Mark Pevey, senior executive director, P–16 Data Management and Operations, University System of Georgia

Clair Pierce (retired), mathematics education specialist on academic standards, Georgia Department of Education

Stephen L. Pruitt, director of academic standards, Georgia Department of Education

Neva Rose, Metropolitan Atlanta Regional P–12 Coordinator, Partnership for Reform In Science and Mathematics (PRISM)

Robert Roy, director, Board of Regents Sponsored Programs, Georgia Institute of Technology

Cheryl Thomas, administrative assistant, P–16 Department, University System of Georgia

Debbie Walker, East Central Georgia Regional P–12 Coordinator, Partnership for Reform In Science and Mathematics (PRISM)

Vannie Walker, Southeast Georgia Regional P–12 Coordinator, Partnership for Reform In Science and Mathematics (PRISM)

# ❶

# A CALL TO ACTION

*Janet S. Kettlewell and Ronald J. Henry*[1]

## INTRODUCTION

There exists significant concern that the U.S. competitive edge in science and technology may be slipping as indicated by low levels of performance of U.S. students on science and mathematics tests compared with non-U.S. students. In his book *The World Is Flat: A Brief History of the Twenty-First Century*, Friedman (2005) adds to the cacophony of voices warning that America is in the midst of a "quiet" crisis.

> We are not producing, in this country, in America, enough young people going into science, technology, and engineering—the fields that are going to be essential for entrepreneurship and innovation in the 21st century.

Multiple blue-ribbon commissions and influential business and national leaders have issued reports on the seriousness of the situation, but little collective effort has been made to advance solutions to the crisis in science, technology, engineering, and mathematics (STEM) fields. In recent years, most of the conversations have been about how higher education can assure that the states and their residents can participate and compete in the knowledge-based global economy.

This book lays out actions that can be taken by K–12 teachers and administrators and by higher education faculty and administrators to contribute to rebuilding America's competitive advantage in science and mathematics. However, it also underscores the point that efforts by individual teachers, schools, faculty, or higher education institutions make little difference unless they are coordinated and integrated with initiatives at higher levels. Thus, this book also lays out actions that must be taken by kindergarten through college leaders and state policy makers if the work is to have lasting positive impact on preparation of our youth for meaningful participation in the twenty-first-century knowledge-based economy.

Over fifty years ago, the launching of the first Earth orbit satellite in 1957 by the Soviet Union propelled the United States into action on STEM issues. Less than a year later, President Eisenhower signed into law the National Defense Education Act, a major part of the effort to restore America's scientific pre-eminence. Its primary focus was on the advancement of student knowledge in mathematics, science, and modern foreign languages. The Business-Higher Education Forum (2006) stated in *Tapping America's Potential: The Education for Innovation Initiative*:

> Today, our nation faces a more serious, if less visible, challenge. One of the pillars of American economic prosperity—our scientific and technological superiority—is beginning to atrophy even as other nations are developing their own human capital. If we wait for a dramatic event—a 21st-century version of Sputnik—it will be too late. There may be no attack, no moment of epiphany, no catastrophe that will suddenly demonstrate the threat. Rather, there will be a slow withering, a gradual decline, a widening gap between a complacent America and countries with the drive, commitment and vision to take our place.

Virtually every major respected organization representing business, research, and education, as well as government science and statistics agencies and commissions, have extensively documented the critical situation in U.S. science, technology, engineering, and mathematics. The Business-Higher Education Forum (2005) recommended in *Commitment to America's Future: Responding to the Crisis in Mathematics and Science*, a kindergarten through college (K–16) approach to resolving the "systemic problems" in science and mathematics, with a concurrent emphasis on K–12 education, higher education, teacher preparation, continued teacher professional learning, and a campaign to raise public awareness as to the severity of the problems.

In another study, Douglass (2006) states the United States now ranks thirteenth in the percent of its population that attends higher education and earns a baccalaureate degree or higher. With reference to STEM fields, this study describes China and India as producing close to a million engineers annually, while the United States and Europe combined produce only about 170,000. Recommendations of the study include a set of "interrelated strategies" that include strengthening preparation for college in K–12 schools, building a "culture of aspirations," and increasing college participation and graduation rates.

A troubling fact is that many of America's parents and students seem unaware of the perilous state of our K–12 educational system, particularly in mathematics and science. The National Center for Education Statistics (2004) report on Trends in International Mathematics and Science Study (TIMSS) conducted over several years indicated that when it comes to self-perception American youth excel.

U.S. high school seniors ranked number one among students from the twenty participating nations in believing that they were doing well in mathematics and number three in agreeing that they were doing well in science. The problem is that in the actual mathematics examination, the same group of students finished eighteenth out of twenty and in the science examination, seventeenth out of twenty.

A more recent survey conducted by the Public Agenda (2007) found that of those respondents expressing an opinion, 62 percent believe that U.S. students are "far behind other countries in mathematics and science." But when asked if their local schools should offer more mathematics and science, 70 percent said, "Things are fine as is." Worse yet, 76 percent of students and 50 percent of parents stated that mathematics and science were irrelevant to the students' lives. Thus, a public awareness campaign is a necessary ingredient for improvements in science and mathematics education to be sustainable.

In the National Academy of Sciences Report (2007), *Rising Above the Gathering Storm: Energizing and Employing America for a Brighter Economic Future*, the highest priority recommendation was to improve K–12 mathematics and science education, principally by producing teachers who have their primary undergraduate degrees in mathematics and science, with a teaching certificate as a secondary but important credential.

In 2002, the National Science Foundation (NSF) launched its Mathematics and Science Partnerships (MSP) initiative as a response to a growing national concern about the educational performance of U.S. children in mathematics and science. It was a comprehensive initiative to produce significant increases in the proportion of the population who have completed programs that equip them with college-level knowledge and skills in STEM fields.

Through MSP, the NSF awarded competitive, merit-based grants to teams composed of institutions of higher education, local K–12 school systems, and their supporting partners. Thus NSF recognized that to solve the nation's problems in STEM fields, it is necessary for K–12 and higher education to work cooperatively in K–16 partnerships.

Since October 2003, the Partnership for Reform In Science and Mathematics (PRISM) has been underway in the state of Georgia. PRISM is a comprehensive research, development and implementation project, funded by the NSF as part of its MSP program. Its focus is to increase the depth of student understanding in science and mathematics. PRISM was designed to test key strategies to increase student learning and achievement in science and mathematics in schools and colleges, to codify what works, to use what works to influence statewide change in policy and practice, and to inform the nation about successes that could be replicated to rebuild America's competitive advantage in science and mathematics.

In this introduction to *Increasing the Competitive Edge in Math and Science*, the principal investigator and co-principal investigator of PRISM set the stage on how to help teachers, faculty, and administrators to rebuild America's competitive advantage in science and mathematics in partnership with state policy makers. Drawing from the research and development within PRISM, and from the research literature, they discuss the conditions and actions that need to be put in place for improvement efforts in STEM fields to be sustainable, and they describe the importance of working simultaneously on sets of interrelated strategies. The authors' on-the-ground insights and tools were learned and developed through PRISM. They are grateful to the National Science Foundation for support of PRISM through award ID 0314953.

## A CALL TO ACTION

Pubic school teachers and administrators, college faculty members and administrators, state policy makers, and business communities all across this nation are urged to respond to this STEM challenge. Rather than responding in disconnected or in idiosyncratic ways, school teachers and administrators, higher education faculty and administrators, policy makers, and the business leaders are urged (1) to "act" on the STEM challenge in kindergarten through college (K–16) partnerships, and (2) to strengthen existing or build new connections between K–16 STEM practices and state policies in science and mathematics.

The reasoning behind a K–16 approach is simple: Science and mathematics practices in K–12 schools affect the subsequent quality of students in higher education, and science and mathematics teacher-preparation programs in higher education affect the quality of science and mathematics teaching in the K–12 schools, which in turn affects children's understanding of science and mathematics as they progress through K–12 schools. The systemic connections between K–12 and higher education are depicted in Figure 1.1, below.

The arrow on the right side of Figure 1.1 depicts the student flow, through the K–12 system and into higher education. The arrow on the left shows the flow of teachers from higher education (where they are prepared) into the schools where they will teach. The ideal is a smooth, almost circular flow connecting both sides of the figure.

The boxes on either side of the figure illustrate how "pieces" of the K–16 education system interact with and determine other pieces. For example, on the right side of Figure 1.1: Science and mathematics course-taking patterns in K–12 are a determinant on the success of these same students later on in college introductory science and mathematics courses. Likewise, student success in these science and mathematics introductory courses is a determinant on the numbers of students who choose and then succeed in STEM majors in college.

On the left side of Figure 1.1, "how" higher education faculty members teach science and mathematics introductory courses is a determinant on the number of college students who pursue science and mathematics teacher-preparation programs and, therefore, on the number of science and mathematics teachers that are prepared. The sustained follow-up of higher education faculty with classroom teachers in professional development, which is of mutual benefit, is also a determinant in the quality of teaching of science and mathematics in the public schools. Moving back to the right side of the figure, the quality of teaching in the public schools, then, is a determinant in K–12 student success in science and mathematics. And so the cycle goes.

While local school-university partnerships can make important in-roads in solving the STEM problems, unless such local partnerships exist in regions of a state where there is a closed loop—with most teachers hired from a single university and most high school graduates in the region attending that same university—the chances for success of local partnerships is greatly enhanced when there is also a state-level K–16 partnership in place through which state policy changes can be introduced and approved to help the innovations introduced by local school-college partners to gain traction.

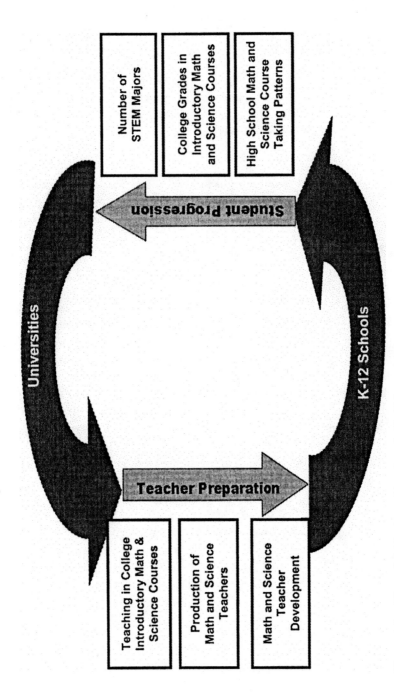

Figure 1.1. Flow of students and teachers in K–16 loop

Through PRISM, Georgia has worked at both the state and regional levels. At the state level, for example, with the Georgia Department of Education taking the lead, K–16 partners have introduced and received approval of policy changes in state K–12 curriculum standards; with the University System of Georgia[2] taking the lead, K–16 partners have introduced and received approval of a new policy that recognizes and rewards faculty for working with the public schools.

These policy changes have served as guideposts—signaling a desired direction for public schools and the colleges and universities within the University System of Georgia on the one hand, and serving as strong motivators and as supports for changing practices in the PRISM regions on the other. The combination of K–16 strategies at regional and state levels in both a top–down and bottom-up approach has contributed significantly to the learning of the K–16 PRISM partners. It has enabled them to contribute to the knowledge base on the teaching and learning of science and mathematics in both K–12 and higher education, and it has made possible the scale-up of many of the PRISM innovations statewide.

There is also a solid literature base supporting K–16, or systemic approaches, to educational reform. The reader is directed to the Web sites[3] of the following organizations for illustrations: The Education Trust, National Association of System Heads, State Higher Education Executive Officers, Education Commission of the States, and Standards-Based Teacher Education Project, a joint project of the Council for Basic Education and the American Association of Colleges for Teacher Preparation.

The Education Trust and others (see for example, Kettlewell et al. 2000) have also documented the importance of pursuing K–16 goals concurrently at local and state levels—local levels to build or strengthen collaborative relationships among arts and sciences, education, and K–12 faculties that are focused on increasing student learning and achievement and that are supported and shared when successful; and state level to create the needed policies, incentives, support, and visibility that make it possible to sustain the reforms once implemented.

## HOW TO GET STARTED

There are many "ways in" to starting or refocusing an existing K–16 partnership on STEM. If the reader is part of either a local or a state-level school-college partnership, one way to get started is for your partnership to analyze your local and state data on science and mathematics student achievement and on science and mathematics teacher preparation. Analysis of baseline data was a first step for Georgia partners when starting PRISM. After analyzing state-level data, Georgia partners looked at school districts that mirrored state demographics and state problems and at universities with the capacity to impact teacher preparation. Fifteen school districts and seven adjacent colleges and universities were invited to participate in PRISM.

Georgia partners also examined policies at the State Board of Education (state governance structure for K–12 policy) and at the Board of Regents (state governance structure for the thirty-five colleges and universities that comprise the University System of Georgia). These analyses revealed the need for a more rigorous science and mathematics K–12 curriculum and the need for explicit incentives for higher education faculty to engage in sustained partnerships with K–12 teachers and administrators toward resolving problems in the STEM pipeline. Based upon these analyses of policy, the decision was made to include the Office of the University System of Georgia and the Georgia Department of Education in the PRISM partnership. All partners agreed to participate.

### Identifying Strategies Already Underway in Your State That Accelerate Progress

Following data analysis, a second step for the reader to consider when increasing the competitive edge in math and science is to take stock of what is already underway in your state that could be built upon. In Georgia, there were two foundational pieces already in place.

### University System of Georgia's P–16 Policy Direction

Since the mid-1990s, under the leadership of the University System of Georgia and the Governor's Office, Georgia had in place fledgling local and state P–16 (pre-school through college) councils. School-college partnership work in the four PRISM regions started in these previously developed local P–16 councils. Thus PRISM partners could build upon the relationships between the schools and colleges that were already under development in their part of the state.

## Board of Regents Policy on Teacher Preparation

PRISM also benefited from the Board of Regents (1998) policy on teacher preparation. Since the Board of Regents is a single governing board for all University System of Georgia institutions, a single policy can quickly shape program redesign, in this case for teacher preparation. This teacher-preparation policy changed the governance structure for teacher preparation from a college of education to a three-way structure involving a college of education, a college of arts and sciences, and partner schools.

Between 1998 and the present, arts and sciences and education faculty in University System institutions that prepare teachers collaborated extensively with the public schools in teacher-preparation program redesign, implementation, program evaluation, and ongoing program modifications to strengthen the quality of teacher preparation. The Standards-Based Teacher Education Project (STEP), a national project of the Council for Basic Education and the American Association of Colleges for Teacher Education, was piloted as a P–16 initiative in Georgia. All four core universities in PRISM participated in STEP, which resulted in an analysis of the arts and sciences and education components of teacher preparation and increased collaboration between the two colleges.

Lessons learned from this prior work in Georgia (described more fully in Henry and Kettlewell, 1999) were used by state and regional partners to design PRISM. One lesson was the importance of bringing together regional P–16 councils periodically to share work, to maintain linkages with directions approved by the State P–16 Council, and for evaluation. A second lesson was the importance of including strategies on both sides of Figure 1.1, already described: A focus on both alignment of challenging courses and curricula, pre-school through college, and on teacher preparation toward practices that improve student learning in K–12 schools. Neither strand without the other is sufficient.

If your state does not yet have a K–16 partnership structure and a three-way collaborative in place for teacher preparation—college of arts and sciences, college of education, and the public schools—either would be a solid place to begin work on *Increasing the Competitive Edge in Math and Science*. In chapter 2 of this book, the reader is given concrete steps on how to build or further develop existing partnerships, such as these two examples from Georgia, and how to transform them into STEM partnerships.

## Research Literature as a Source for Elements of Your STEM Initiative Design

A summary of relevant research is given here to help the reader identify research-based strategies for inclusion in the design of a STEM initiative in your state.

*Challenging Courses.*    The Education Trust (2000) describes completion of challenging courses as one of two key leverage points for increasing student achievement. The science courses a student takes can exert a "strong and statistically significant influence" on achievement in science (Schneider et al. 1997, 37). Schneider et al. found that the science courses taken in high school were a better predictor of college entrance than family background effects. They also found that the ability level of the class was not as important as the progression along a sequence of science courses. If your state does not already require all students to complete a rigorous secondary course sequence in science and mathematics that is aligned with freshman courses in college, including this dimension in your STEM initiative design is highly recommended. More detail on development of K–12 challenging courses and curricula is discussed in chapter 3.

*Expert Teachers.*    In order for K–12 students to experience challenging curricula, Darling-Hammond and Post (2000) argue that expert teachers are required. They note that students in high minority schools have less than a 50 percent chance of getting a licensed science and mathematics teacher with a degree in the field in which he or she is teaching.

> Recent studies have found that the difference in teacher quality may represent the single most important school resource differential between minority and white children and that it explains at least as much of the variance in student achievement as socioeconomic status. (Darling-Hammond and Post 2000, 128)

The groundbreaking research of Sanders and others confirms the crucial role of the teacher in increasing student achievement. Sanders and Rivers (1996) used value-added methods to examine the cumulative effects of teacher quality on academic achievement. The effectiveness of all mathematics teachers in grades 3, 4, and 5 in two large metropolitan school districts in Tennessee was estimated by determining the average amount of annual growth of the students in their classrooms. These data were used to identify the most effective (top 20 percent) and the least effective (bottom 20 percent) teachers.

The progress of children assigned to these low- and high-performing teachers was tracked over a three-year period. Children assigned to three effective teachers in a row scored at the 83rd percentile in mathematics at the end of fifth grade, while children assigned to three ineffective teachers in a row scored at the twenty-ninth percentile. Similarly, Rivkin et al. (1998) used Texas data to replicate the research of Sanders and Rivers and demonstrated that the influence of teachers on student achievement is far greater than any other variable.

If your state has shortages in science and mathematics teachers, if the ethnic background of your teachers does not mirror that of the student body, and if elementary and middle school teachers in your state have less than rigorous content backgrounds in science and mathematics, the authors strongly recommend inclusion of work on teacher quality, quantity, and diversity in your STEM initiative design. The reader is referred to chapters 5, 6, and 7 for more detail on specific strategies to increase teacher quality, quantity, and diversity in science and mathematics.

***How People Learn.*** Research findings suggest that students at all levels build new knowledge and understanding on what they already know and believe. Particularly in science, many students have preconceptions that are inconsistent with accepted, extant science knowledge. Students often hold on tenaciously to these ideas, which can be resistant to change, particularly when conventional teaching strategies are used (Wandersee et al. 1994).

Students change their ideas when they discover alternatives that seem plausible and appear to be more useful (Hewson and Thorley 1989). Learning can be enhanced when students have opportunities to articulate their ideas to others, challenge each other's ideas, and, in doing so, reconstruct their own ideas (Rosebery et al. 1992). Effective learning requires students to take control of their own learning. Thus, opportunities for self-assessment in science and mathematics need to be provided so that students can understand the main purposes of their learning and thereby grasp what they need to do to achieve (Black and Wiliam 1998).

For mathematics, research findings suggest that mathematical proficiency is developed through five interdependent strands: conceptual understanding, procedural fluency, strategic competence, adaptive reasoning, and productive disposition (Kilpatrick et al. 2001). Effective programs of teacher preparation and professional development help teachers understand the mathematics they teach, how their students learn that mathematics, and how to facilitate that learning.

Teachers adapt what they are learning to deal with problems that arise in their own teaching. Mathematics understanding is facilitated best when students have direct experience with methods and processes of inquiry. Tasks are central to students' learning—students learn best when they are presented with academically challenging work that focuses on sense making and problem solving as well as skill building.

For science and mathematics, the seminal book by Bransford el al. (1999) entitled *How People Learn* summarizes key research findings as follows: (1) "Students come to the classroom with preconceptions about how the world works. If their initial understanding is not engaged, they may fail to grasp the new concepts and information that are taught, or they may learn them for the purposes of a test but revert to their preconceptions outside the classroom" (14). (2) "To develop competence in an area of inquiry, students must: (a) have a deep foundation of factual knowledge; (b) understand facts and ideas in the context of a conceptual framework; and (c) organize knowledge in ways that facilitate retrieval and application" (16). (3) "A 'meta-cognitive' approach to instruction can help students learn to take control of their own learning by defining learning goals and monitoring their progress in achieving them" (18).

It is well-established that teachers' deep understanding of science and mathematics content has a significant impact on what K–12 students learn (Darling-Hammond and Post 2000). Yet, requiring a teacher to major in science or mathematics does not necessarily prepare them to be effective teachers—the correlation between number of content courses and teacher effectiveness is unclear (Wilson et al. 2001). A difficult challenge is the concordance among the teaching methods and strategies used in content courses, those used in pedagogy courses, and those that teacher candidates are taught to use to teach content to their K–12 pupils.

Similar challenges hold for teacher professional development. To be effective, such development must be tied to student learning content standards and classroom instruction, sustained over time, connected with higher education, and must be a part of a larger effort to improve instruction. Professional development must also be intentional, ongoing, and systemic (Guskey 2000). To sustain reforms, teachers need to be engaged in inquiry and receive systemic support by committed leadership (National Research Council 1999).

Many science and mathematics faculty members are not prepared for teaching in ways that allow students to develop deep understanding. Many faculty members teach the way they were taught, without the same level of insightful questioning and collaborative efforts that characterize their research.

Implications for teaching from *How People Learn* are (1) "Teachers must draw out and work with the preexisting understandings that their students bring with them" (19); (2) "Teachers must teach some subject matter in depth, providing many examples in which the same concept is at work and providing a firm foundation for factual knowledge" (20); and (3) "The teaching of meta-cognitive skills should be integrated into the curriculum in a variety of subject areas" (21).

The challenge is to modify or develop courses in which current and aspiring K–12 teachers of science and mathematics are taught using methods that follow sound research findings. Since understanding science is more than knowing facts, and mathematical proficiency is more than mastering a skill to carry out procedures accurately, teacher candidates need learning environments that facilitate proficiency and understanding (National Research Council 1999). What teachers are taught and how they are taught is important. In all science and mathematics courses for aspiring and in-service K–12 teachers of science and mathematics, science and mathematics faculties should model the best teaching practices.

If not already in place in the schools and colleges in your state, it is strongly recommended that you incorporate these research findings into your STEM initiative design of teacher professional learning, teacher preparation, and strategies to encourage higher education faculty to provide a more college-student-centered learning environment—an important lever for increasing both the number of STEM majors in college and the number of college students who aspire to become science and mathematics teachers. Again, there is much more detail on specific strategies given in chapters 5, 6, and 7.

*Learning Communities.* Dewey (1933) in the 1920s and 1930s gave rise to the concept of a student learning community. Dewey advocated learning that was active, student-centered, and involved shared inquiry. A combination of these approaches in the late 1970s and 1980s produced a pedagogy and structure that has led, among other things, to students' increased grade point averages, retention, and intellectual development. In college, a number of institutions use learning communities to help students in their first year (Freshman Learning Communities [FLCs]) by placing some students in groups that take the same courses together. The idea is to help students connect better with college by providing them with a space to learn together across courses. Students who join FLCs have much higher retention in college than those who do not join (Hotchkiss et al. 2006).

Many K–12 school reform efforts in the United States have achieved less than optimal results over the years because reformers have underestimated the complexity of changing a system so large, varied, and conservative. Most reforms have not been aimed at fundamental issues of teaching and learning. Instead, they have been focused on doing more of the same with greater intensity: more hours, more work, more tests; or they have focused on non-academic concerns such as discipline or parental involvement. This realization led in part to advocacy of teacher professional learning communities (DuFour and Eaker 1998). A professional learning community model is built on the four pillars of mission, vision, values, and goals. Importantly, the main activities of the teams in this model are collective inquiry and action research.

Senge et al. (2000) and Wheatley (2002) emphasize the need to learn and practice new behaviors to promote collective learning. Learning communities are "spaces" where people from different perspectives learn more powerfully in concert with others who are struggling with the same issues. A learning community provides a safe environment where trust is engendered, people feel connected, and hierarchies are leveled.

In college, some faculty have formed communities of practice (Wenger et al. 2002) or faculty learning communities (Cox and Richlin 2004) around common issues with which they are dealing. For example, one interdisciplinary group meets to discuss how to improve learning in courses that have section sizes greater than 100 or a research group of faculty, graduate students, and undergraduate students meets regularly to discuss progress in various experiments they are conducting.

PRISM emphasizes learning communities to provide a mechanism through which college faculty and school teachers together could learn, share, research, and document the best practices of cognitive sciences, science education research, and practitioners in teaching and learning of science and mathematics. The learning communities provide a forum for analyzing existing performance data and planning for instruction based on the analysis. One potential value of a learning community is as a form of professional development.

Professional development should be designed to develop the capacity of faculty to work collectively on problems of practice, within their own institutions and with practitioners from other institutions, as much as to support the knowledge and skill development of individual educators. This view derives from the assumption that learning is essentially a collaborative, rather than an individual, activity—that educators learn more powerfully in concert with others who are struggling with the same problems—and that the essential purpose of professional development should be the improvement of student learning, not just the improvement of faculty who are involved in the professional development activity.

If not already in place in the schools and colleges in your state, it is strongly recommended that you include learning communities in your STEM initiative. More detail on successful implementation of learning communities is given in chapter 6.

*Public Awareness.* A Public Agenda (2006) report found that the number of parents who worry about whether local schools are teaching enough mathematics and science declined from 52 percent in 1994 to 32 percent in 2006. Another Public Agenda (2007) report finds that while parents are aware of the importance of more mathematics and science in the preparation of students, they still remain complacent. Satisfaction with teachers and curriculum underlies parents' complacency, with only one-third regarding improvements in mathematics and science as an urgent priority.

Students also pay lip service to the importance of taking higher levels of mathematics and science courses since most students experience these subject areas as profoundly uninteresting and largely irrelevant to their futures. The 2007 report recommends addressing this "urgency gap" between leaders and experts on the one hand and parents and students on the other.

Research shows that increasing public awareness on education issues can make a difference. In the early 1990s, advocates for increasing education standards began a movement toward "algebra for all."[4] Public Agenda (2007) notes that this emphasis has paid off with eight of ten parents now viewing algebra to be essential for student success. Parents and students need to be made aware of the background needed for success in the current and future job market. While the job market is much broader in scope than careers in STEM fields, most careers still need a strong science and mathematics grounding.

The U.S. Department of Education (2000) identified sixteen career clusters which group occupations and broad industries based on commonalities and identify pathways from high school to two- and four-year colleges, graduate school and the workplace. The clusters help students focus on an area of interest or possible career path without confining them to preparation for a specific job.

The National Association of State Directors of Career Technical Education Consortium (2006), a consortium for innovative career and workforce development resources, developed sample plans of study for grades 9–12 that match the demands of the sixteen career clusters, including a sequence of recommended core courses and high school electives. Their recommendations call for four years of science for fourteen of the total sixteen career clusters, with the remaining two clusters calling for three years.

PRISM includes a strategy to increase public awareness as to the benefits of all students meeting higher K–12 standards in science and mathematics, and the consequences of not meeting them. If a public awareness campaign is not already in place in your state, its inclusion in your STEM initiative design is strongly recommended. Specific strategies about public awareness are elaborated on in chapter 4.

*Administrative Support.*   The National Research Council (1999) suggested four strategies that administrators could use to encourage higher education faculty to learn new effective approaches to teaching and then apply them: (1) Provide faculty with the resources required to consult with colleagues and education experts; (2) establish a centralized fund for educational improvement in the dean's office that can send a powerful message regarding a change in departmental values; (3) favor in promotion, tenure, and salary deliberations, faculty work that engages students in innovative courses; and (4) advocate for the use of innovative design and assessment of courses and research focused on teaching and learning in the discipline as evidence of a faculty member's productivity as a teacher-scholar.

PRISM included a strategy to consider policy and practice changes in roles and rewards for higher education faculty involved in K–16 activities. In addition, another PRISM strategy examined teacher working conditions that would support and encourage teachers to become the experts necessary to bring all students to high standards of learning. If these elements are not already in place in your state, their inclusion into your STEM initiative design is strongly recommended.

## DEVELOPING YOUR STEM INITIATIVE DESIGN

From Figure 1.1, described previously, from the above discussions about the importance of analyzing state and local data and about taking inventory of related initiatives already underway, and from reviewing the research literature, the reader in partnership with others should be ready to identify many of the key dimensions that need to be emphasized in a STEM initiative design in your state and in different regions of your state. While there are certainly variations in student achievement data and in teacher preparation from state to state, given the national picture within the United

States discussed at the beginning of this chapter, a suggested over-all goal for all states when increasing the competitive edge in math and science is to increase student achievement in science and mathematics, kindergarten through college, while closing achievement gaps among various demographic groups. Georgia's design included two groups of interrelated strategies.

Group I was to advance student progression, through: (1) Increasing public awareness as to the need for all K–12 students to have access to, to be prepared for, and to succeed in challenging courses and curricula in science and mathematics; (2) raising and aligning student learning standards in science and mathematics for K–12 schools with expectations for college entry; and (3) engaging college faculty in changing how science and mathematics are taught so as to influence college student success in science and mathematics introductory courses so that more students continue to major and graduate with STEM degrees and more choose to become future science and mathematics teachers.

Group II was to improve teaching quality in the schools, through: (1) Increasing the number and quality of new science and mathematics teachers prepared; (2) influencing high school and college students to become science and mathematics teachers; (3) increasing current elementary teachers' content knowledge in science and mathematics; (4) engaging higher education faculty in teaching science and mathematics in ways that engage elementary teachers; (5) increasing teaching quality in science and mathematics in the fifteen PRISM school districts; (6) engaging school and college faculty together in professional learning that focuses on increasing student learning and achievement in science and mathematics at all levels of the educational continuum, kindergarten through college (K–16 learning communities); (7) initiating new policies that provide incentives and improved working conditions for teaching science and mathematics in K–12 schools, to reduce teacher attrition; and (8) providing a reward structure in colleges and universities to encourage faculty members to sustain involvement in improving science and mathematics teaching and learning in K–12 schools.

These interrelated PRISM strategies were designed to achieve three goals:

Goal 1: Raise expectations and achievement in science and mathematics in K–12 schools, while closing achievement gaps among demographic groups by providing challenging science and mathematics curricula and materials for all students; and by raising the awareness of students, parents, and the community of the need for all K–12 students to complete challenging courses and curricula in science and mathematics.

Goal 2: Raise student achievement in science and mathematics in K–12 schools through increasing and sustaining the number, quality, and diversity of K–12 teachers teaching science and mathematics by providing high-quality professional development to current K–12 teachers who teach science and mathematics; by strengthening the content and pedagogy in science and mathematics for pre-service teachers; by ensuring a sufficient pipeline of highly qualified and diverse science and mathematics teachers to meet demand; and by providing incentives for teacher assignment and retention to ensure access to highly qualified and experienced science and mathematics teachers by students who need them most.

Goal 3: Raise student achievement in science and mathematics in K–12 schools through increasing the responsiveness of higher education to the needs of K–12 schools by increasing the participation of science and mathematics faculty in teacher preparation and professional development; and by providing incentives for science and mathematics faculty members to engage in research with K–12 schools on effective practices in science and mathematics.

**Logic Model**

As partners at the state and regional levels engage in development of STEM Initiative Designs all across the United States, each needs a mechanism to monitor progress and to track momentum. Because *Increasing the Competitive Edge in Math and Science* is a long-term proposition, each state and local partnership needs to be able to answer questions such as the following: How do you know if you are on course? What "leading indicators" are acceptable to you as evidence of progress? How do you know that success on your leading indicators results in your ultimate goal—increased student achievement in science and mathematics while closing achievement gaps among demographic groups?

In PRISM, the Georgia partnership adopted the logic model defined in Figure 1.2 through which to answer these kinds of questions.

The PRISM Leadership Team first established a sound partnership and began collaboration on the development of needed policies. As PRISM activities have been implemented, through use of evaluation data, the Leadership Team has monitored participation of K–12 and higher education partners. As implementation has increased, the Leadership Team has analyzed

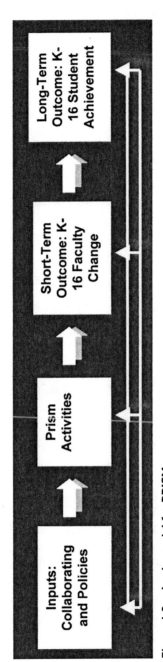

Figure I.2.  Logic model for PRISM

evaluation data for indications of changed behavior in school and college classrooms of PRISM participants. Finally, the PRISM partnership has analyzed the effects of changed classroom behavior on the part of teachers and faculty on improvements in student learning.

## Pulling the Pieces Together

When increasing the competitive edge in math and science, it is important to remember the limits to reform. Zemsky (2008), in an article on reform in college, commented on two important principles spelled out by Massy et al. (2007). First, improvement is about making things better, not about fixing things that have gone wrong. Second, the key agents of change are necessarily the faculty. However, while these are necessary principles, they are not sufficient. The challenge is to institutionalize the change. On this score education in general has a very bad history.

Another challenge is that even if change in a school or college is institutionalized, how do you bring it to scale across a state or group of states? There needs to be some agency within and across the state that embraces the reform and supports it financially. Having the necessary innovations created and developed by teachers, faculty, and administrators is a necessary condition for reform—the sufficient condition is a sustaining demand within K–16 education for the kind of change business and government leaders have sought from education in order to rebuild America's competitive advantage in science and mathematics. To date, as Zemsky (2008) notes, that is something that no amount of strong language or heartfelt lamentation or governmental jawboning has succeeded in producing.

In Georgia, PRISM partners have embraced the above two principles by involving teachers and faculty in making things better. In subsequent chapters the authors describe actions that teachers, faculty, and administrators can take at the local level. They also describe actions that must be taken by K–16 leaders and policy makers if the improvements are to be institutionalized and brought to scale across a state. This book represents our attempt to share with others lessons learned in PRISM. The authors hope it also serves as a call to action—a catalyst for developing new or enhancing existing partnerships—toward resolving the systemic problems in STEM fields in the United States.

The remaining chapters go into detail on strategies and tools to be followed to help states rebuild America's competitive advantage in science and mathematics. In chapter 2, the reader learns how to build effective partnerships and how to design effective STEM initiatives in your state that make possible local actions that can be taken by teachers and administrators while building coordinated and interrelated strategies that link with state efforts. The reader also learns how to identify conditions for success and how to sustain them over time.

In chapters 3 and 4, the reader learns strategies for linking local curriculum development efforts in science and mathematics with state curricular frameworks; how to engage higher education in the process so that the knowledge and skills expected of students in high school clearly aligns with expectations for college and work; and how to increase student, parent, and community interest in all students taking more rigorous science and mathematics courses. As in chapter 2, conditions for success and sustainability are identified.

In chapters 5 and 6, the reader learns successful strategies for engaging K–12 teachers of science and mathematics in continued professional learning; and how K–16 professional learning communities help to sustain and accelerate the content and pedagogical knowledge of K–12 science and mathematics teachers and the pedagogical knowledge of scientists and mathematicians in higher education. As in previous chapters, the authors emphasize the conditions for success and sustainability of these strategies.

In chapter 7, the reader learns successful strategies for engaging higher education faculty in K–16 improvement in STEM education fields. Particular actions are described in this chapter that may be taken by higher education faculty and administrators, actions such as improvement of introductory science and mathematics courses; involvement of science and mathematics faculty in teacher preparation; the importance of increasing college graduation rates in science and mathematics fields; actions to be taken by higher education leaders and state policy makers; and finally, conditions for success and sustainability of these strategies.

As in all large-scale change strategies—particularly one with needed local or regional strategies as well as state strategies—it is important for the reader to conceptualize clearly an integrated and coherent evaluation design that includes all aspects of *Increasing the Competitive Edge in Math and Science*. In chapter 8, the reader learns how to design and implement a comprehensive evaluation and learns how evaluation can be used to promote continuous improvement and sustainability.

In chapter 9, the reader is able to see an overall focus on sustainability—that pulls together elements from all of the previous chapters—making clear the actions to be taken by teachers and administrators in K–12 schools and school districts, actions needed by faculty and administrators in higher education, and actions needed by state policy makers. Finally, the reader is able to see an overall summary of steps necessary for success in chapter 10. The authors invite your participation in this work, and in this call to action they implore local, regional, and state partners to accept the STEM challenge and to move forward with urgency.

## NOTES

1. Janet S. Kettlewell is the principal investigator in the Partnership for Reform In Science and Mathematics (PRISM), a systemic K–16 STEM initiative in Georgia. She is the vice chancellor for P–16 Initiatives for the University System of Georgia in Atlanta. Ronald J. Henry is the co-principal investigator in the Partnership for Reform In Science and Mathematics (PRISM), a systemic K–16 STEM initiative in Georgia. He is a physicist, provost, and senior vice president for Academic Affairs at Georgia State University in Atlanta.

2. The University System of Georgia includes thirty-five colleges and universities governed by a single Board of Regents. It includes two-year colleges and all baccalaureate, masters, and doctoral degree-granting pubic universities in Georgia.

3. Websites of cited organizations: The Education Trust, http://www2.edtrust .org/edtrust/default; National Association of System Heads, http://www.nashonline .org/content/k-16info.html; State Higher Education Executive Officers, http:// www.sheeo.org; Education Commission of the States, http://www.ecs.org; Standards-Based Teacher Education Project, http://www.aacte.org/index.php?/Programs/ Standards-and-Practice-STEP/standards-based-teacher-education-project-stepr.html.

4. For example, see Steen (1999).

# PARTNERSHIPS NEEDED TO INCREASE THE COMPETITIVE EDGE IN MATH AND SCIENCE

*Nancy Vandergrift and Sheila Jones*[1]

## INTRODUCTION

The future of American youth is in jeopardy in science, technology, engineering, and mathematics (STEM). No one person or organization has the key to solving the crisis in America about current levels of student achievement in STEM. Partnerships are needed that focus on improving science and mathematics student learning, kindergarten through college (K–16). Core educational organizations that represent the K–16 STEM pipeline must collaborate in development of solutions. And solutions cannot only be crafted locally. If reform is to be sustainable, a large-scale approach is necessary.

This chapter describes strategies to strengthen existing STEM partnerships and to establish new ones in order to build a base upon which to launch an educational reform initiative or project focused on improving science and mathematics student achievement. Individual or small group efforts at improving student learning, while remarkable and perhaps successful, have been historically unsustainable over time. Suggestions are made on how to expand small partnerships into large-scale initiatives that break down cultural barriers to resolve systemic problems. If improving STEM education is a national imperative as stated in *Rising Above the Gathering Storm* (National Academy of Sciences 2007), and you are heeding the call to action by reading this book, then it is critical to ensure your project makes a difference by developing and nurturing a results-oriented partnership.

Specific examples are taken from the successful National Science Foundation Math and Science Partnership (MSP) grant called Partnership for Reform in Science and Mathematics, or PRISM for short. PRISM is a comprehensive project whose partnerships ran the gamut from state policy makers (University System of Georgia and the Georgia Department of Education) working together to roll out a new K–12 state curriculum to school districts partnering as a region to offer professional learning, as well as to classroom-based learning communities of teachers analyzing student data to develop common assessments.

A primary emphasis on developing and maintaining PRISM partnerships was due to the fact that partnerships were required for external funding. Therefore, to achieve the PRISM goal of improving science and mathematics student achievement, PRISM needed to create well-defined partnerships. Early actions were based on prior experience with preschool through college council collaborations.[2] Some decisions were deliberate and backed by research. Many lessons were learned the hard way: by trial and error. Other lessons were successes that spread throughout the partnership so that no one really remembered how the idea occurred. PRISM partners share challenges and successes in hopes they may be helpful to the reader as you build or enrich existing partnerships toward a shared goal of increasing student achievement in science and mathematics, kindergarten through college.

## WHY PARTNERSHIPS?

The use of partnerships to initiate and to expand educational reform has become a defining feature of many twenty-first-century initiatives. Research shows that partnerships add value and create positive outcomes for all partners (Scherer 2006). In fact, establishing partnerships has become a required program component in educational reform proposals by many federal granting agencies and private foundations (for example, Title II of No Child Left Behind [NCLB] 2002 and the National Science Foundation [NSF] Math and Science Partnership Programs 2002). So, whether or not one believes partnerships are of value, there is great interest in demonstrating for grantors that a partnership is in place when applying for funding.

Collaboration is also a concept that is increasingly evident among K–12 teachers. The education community has embraced collaboration as professional development by creating school-based learning groups, such as the professional learning communities being promoted by DuFour and Eaker (1998). In a broad-based systemic approach, K–16 councils (for example, Education Trust 2000) are based on creating working relationships among educators ranging from kindergarten through college (K–16) at local as well as state levels as a viable way to improve teaching and learning.

Since the crisis in STEM education in America is real in both K–12 schools and in colleges and universities, it is systemic. Collaboration is needed at all levels of the educational continuum, K–16. Working at reform in both state-level (top-down) and local-level (bottom-up) combinations has been shown to be an effective strategy. School-university partnerships can contribute significantly to improving STEM education as long as the members of the different cultures understand each other. Along the way, appreciation and trust are earned from sharing the work and listening to each other. High regard is also earned when learning about other partners' working conditions under organizational and policy constraints not familiar to the other partner's culture.

The gold standard in these partnerships is to keep the conversations and efforts focused on improving student learning and achievement. How does one develop a conducive environment to help partnerships achieve a high level of trust and understanding as well as ensure the work is of high quality and all members' contributions are valued?

## Create Strong Leadership at Every Level

There are many "ways in" to starting or refocusing an existing K–16 partnership on STEM. One of the first steps in your partnership-building process is to choose key personnel with interest and enthusiasm in Increasing the Competitive Edge in Math and Science. Search for promising projects and collaborations already in progress; people from these groups can make excellent partners and may already be working toward at least one common goal. It is important to choose partners in a deliberate and purposeful manner to bring together expertise and authority from core educational organizations and institutions. It is necessary to have representation from every key institution and organization in the composition of leadership teams at every level, including a core leadership team. Partners must work cooperatively toward common goals and ensure accountability, so be sure that your project's goals are clear.

You should limit membership in your core leadership team to those key personnel with authority to make decisions concerning the redirection of resources. Key personnel must also be able to commit their institution or organization to work toward a common mission and goals. Representation from public schools, universities (in the STEM disciplines), policy makers, administrators, as well as key business and community members should comprise your core leadership team. Your core leadership team should meet regularly and communicate as often as possible via e-mail, telephone, and face-to-face visits between meetings.

## ORIGINS OF THE PRISM PARTNERSHIP

In Georgia, where PRISM was based, preexisting networks had been established in the 1990s through the statewide Georgia P–16 council and local and regional P–16 councils. Using P–16 collaboration as a foundation for partnership reform efforts, other collaborative activities were initiated over subsequent years and continued sporadically. This long history of partnership and collaboration in Georgia demonstrated to educators, administrators, and policy makers that goals could be achieved using partnerships.

In 2002, the University System of Georgia (USG) P–16 department issued a call for participation to partner in the development of a grant proposal in response to the National Science Foundation Math and Science Partnership Program request for proposals. The invitation went to the fifteen USG higher education institutions that had teacher-preparation programs. Eventually, four regional teams that represented Georgia's unique demographic, geographic, and cultural diversity were invited to participate. Each region had as its core partner a higher education institution and local partner school districts that had agreed to work with them.

At the kick-off meeting in 2003, the four regions had in place loosely formed groups of individuals representing key stakeholders. Some educational units and individuals had little or no history of working together. All in all, the PRISM "partnership" was comprised of a group of people from different backgrounds and working cultures with different levels of collaborative experience.

Although developing a strong leadership team at the state level was of critical importance, it was also necessary to create collaborative teams out of the loosely formed groups that populated the initiative in its early stages. Regional, district, and classroom-based (e.g., professional learning communities) partnerships were developed in tandem due to the pressing nature of grant work. PRISM designed the partnerships with overlapping membership at all levels to create a two-way pipeline that served to spread the vision and goals and ensure accountability at all levels. See Figure 2.1 for a schematic of the PRISM partnership(s). (In figure 2.1, IHE stands for institute of higher education.)

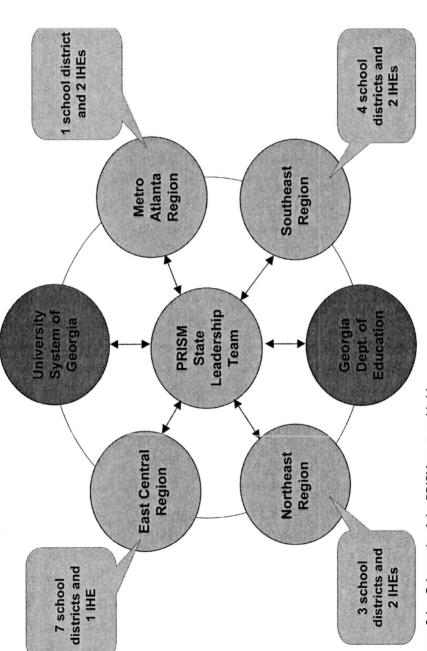

**Figure 2.1. Schematic of the PRISM partnership(s)**

Representatives from core partners formed a PRISM state leadership team whose purpose was not only to oversee implementation of the project, but to lead by example through the expansion of the roles of K–12 educators and higher education faculty. Through early efforts of working together, one of the first lessons learned was that K–16 partnerships must learn from one another. In particular, partners need to build the trust necessary to challenge each other's thinking so that decisions lead not just to activities but to achievement of goals (Winkler and Fretchling 2005). In the four PRISM regions, partners created regional partnerships called Regional Coordinating Committees (RCC) to design and implement the work. The state leadership team worked closely with the four regional partnerships to promote reform and achieve the PRISM goals.

## CREATE JOINT LEADERSHIP

Strong leadership is needed to build mutual trust among partners and encourage regional members to be responsible for the work. With diverse institutions and a variety of educational cultures populating a partnership, your challenge is to form leadership teams with understanding of and respect for all the complexities of each stakeholder's culture within the diverse educational institutions. One strategy is to create joint leadership, with leaders who agree to hold themselves responsible and accountable for contributing to common goals.

If multiple regions are involved in your STEM initiative, it may be tempting to leave the structure of regional leadership teams up to each individual region. This works up to a point. Based upon lessons learned through PRISM, at a minimum, regional partnerships must include representation from three key stakeholder groups: college of arts and sciences, college of education, and K–12 public schools. In addition, regional partnerships focused on increasing student achievement in science and mathematics should be jointly led by a three-person team with one member representing each of these three key stakeholder groups.

*Example: Core PRISM Leadership Team.* A strong top-tier PRISM leadership triad included the Principal Investigator (PI) who represented Education, the Co-Principal Investigator (Co-PI) who represented Arts and Sciences (both in higher education), and the Project Director who was originally a public school teacher. They worked in collaboration to shape a cooperative leadership model that would embrace and uphold the values of the PRISM partnership, as well as assume the responsibility of implementing the work at the regional level in the same collaborative manner. The PRISM core leaders saw the potential for sharing authority and nurturing leadership qualities in the members of PRISM (Wolff 2001). Without these three individuals, successful collaborative partnerships would never have occurred.

## DEVELOP EXPERIENCE IN COLLABORATION

If your partnership is to be successful in responding to the STEM crisis and working toward a comprehensive goal such as improving K–16 science and mathematics achievement, then members must be able to collaborate productively. If real change is to occur, it is important for members of the partnership not to fall back on the status quo of solitary or compartmentalized efforts. This may happen if you assume that all partners know how to collaborate.

It is necessary for partnerships to take the time and effort from the outset so the leadership team builds understanding and experience in working collaboratively. This is a challenge, particularly in the beginning because there are so many competing start-up activities. When the levels of experience in collaboration vary among members, it can pose particular problems of differing expectations. However, it is critically important to spend the necessary time to ensure that your partners grow to trust and respect each other enough to work together. Communication is also a key to building a collaborative mindset.

When some members of a leadership team have little or no experience in how to collaborate, a challenge is to help them build capacity. You may want to focus the majority of an early leadership team meeting on learning about each other's culture, sharing opinions, and forming a collective idea of roles and responsibilities. Consensus-building is a key strategy to forming common understandings and mutual trust. You may find that your leadership team would benefit from participating in training on partnership development. In PRISM, a well-known partnership expert helped Georgia's leadership team strengthen skills needed to cultivate effective partnerships.

It is also important for partners to meet regularly. Holding monthly leadership team meetings is recommended so that partners keep the conversations going and maintain high interest. Early in the work of a partnership it is important to make organizational work a priority. Development of implementation plans with categories for responsibilities and timelines for accountability is highly recommended.

If you build a two-tiered structure—a state-level and regional-level K–16 leadership team—you are likely to find that discussions about state-level implementation plans are very helpful as partners return to their regions and, in turn, develop structures and begin to implement strategies.

In addition to monthly meetings, an annual retreat is highly recommended. A longer block of time helps your leadership team have in-depth discussions about its progress toward annual and long-range goals as well as to finalize goals and objectives for the next year. Through participation in annual retreats, you also should find a growing spirit of camaraderie develops among the participants that can lead to team stability.

***Example: Collaboration in a PRISM Region.*** In one PRISM region, participants used the language of collaboration, "we," to talk about decision-making, planning, implementing activities, and assessing progress. Through substantial collaboration, educators had formed a better understanding of each other's expertise and interests, formed mutual trust, and felt comfortable in communicating. The use of "partnership language" and the growth of collegial interpersonal relationships were indicators of partnership stability in this region.

## Recommended Examples of PRISM Partnership Structures and Their Evolution

In each of the four regions, a leadership group was formed called a Regional Coordinating Committee (RCC). The purpose of the RCC was to design, implement, and coordinate work across all partner school districts in each region, as well as coordinate activity at the higher education institution level. Teachers-in-residence, called K–12 coordinators, worked with the university leaders to form a joint leadership triad. Along with directing the work of the RCCs, they were also members of the state leadership team.

The RCC was comprised of these regional leaders; school district specialists in teacher professional learning and the liaisons to the teachers; Lead Teachers (the school- and classroom-based teacher leaders); and higher education faculty interested in improving instruction and student learning in college as well as in K–12. Meeting once per month, these partnerships set their own agenda within the parameters of PRISM goals to ensure decisions were results-oriented. Early regional efforts focused on building capacity for communicating to promote PRISM's vision, and empowering individuals to make connections with others to improve the quality of science and mathematics teaching and learning.

The PRISM project director (state-level) attended all RCC meetings and worked with regional leaders to ensure that the meetings were collaborative as well as compatible with the PRISM vision. Due to the participation of the project director at all four regions' RCC meetings, ideas could be shared across regions and PRISM was assured of better communication. The project director's participation also brought verification that these meetings were important.

The following examples of two PRISM RCCs may help make clear how partnerships may grow to become accomplished collaboratives while trying to effect change.

One PRISM RCC began as a very eclectic group of professional educators and representatives from the community. Superintendents, curriculum directors, principals, teachers, and university professors were involved along with community people who saw PRISM as a connection to work they were interested in doing.

In the first two years, the RCC functioned as a leadership team charting the course for the PRISM work in the region based on needs of their partner institutions of higher education and partner school districts determined through the analyses of science and mathematics student and teacher data. The RCC also spent time learning about each partner by visiting each other's institutions (schools and colleges). Gradually as the work continued, the balance of the work shifted from determining and guiding the work, to sharing each other's successes and learning from the work done regionally and within each institution.

Another PRISM RCC consisted largely of educators and administrators from each of the participating school districts and institutions of higher education. While the diversity of the membership of the RCC remained constant, the work changed significantly as the project gathered momentum and the participants viewed themselves as integral members of a valuable and sustainable partnership. Initial tasks of the RCC were heavily organizational in nature.

When project implementation began, the main role of the RCC was to provide support and leadership for the developing learning communities in the region. (You can learn more about learning communities in chapter 6). Meetings took on the structure of participant presentations and small group sharing sessions. Soon thereafter, a core group of PRISM participants began to see the impact in their schools and departments and became strong advocates for the program. With this momentum created, the role of the RCC changed once again. The group evolved into a regional learning community where participants not only supported each other's work, but also learned together, engaged in collaborative inquiry, assessed regional progress, and challenged each other to work toward sustainability.

## Recommendations

Based on lessons learned in PRISM: (1) regional partnerships should meet regularly, at least monthly, in the first year in order to build capacity for collaboration; (2) the person responsible for coordinating the STEM initiative at the state level should participate in the regional meetings; and (3) if you have local partnerships in a region, then the regional coordinator needs to attend the local partnership meetings on a regular basis.

You should find that regional partnerships become important mechanisms for promoting the vision and mission of your STEM initiative, for advocating change, and for building sustainability for the work. You also should find that over time each regional partnership may take on different characteristics, with unique strengths and challenges. That is okay, so long as your work focuses concurrently on continuing to strengthen your partnerships and on improving student academic achievement. Both must be apparent in the earliest interactions at all levels.

In addition to your regional partnership meeting regularly and building trust, partners need to analyze their local data on science and mathematics student achievement and on science and mathematics teachers. As time progresses you are likely to find that your regional partnerships are sharing each other's successes and learning from the work done regionally and within each school and university.

## ACHIEVE YOUR GOALS GIVEN UNIQUE CULTURES

No one person or organization has the key to solving the crisis of improving student achievement in STEM. A multi-faceted solution requires a variety of expertise and skills. Individual, interpersonal relationships cannot sustain reform efforts; neither can one rely on adding goals to pre-existing partnerships (Scherer 2006, 10) and achieve long-lasting reform. One benefit of a K–16 partnership is that it brings together partners with common goals and an array of expertise to tackle the STEM crisis. A challenge is to plan activities that are successfully implemented across the different institutions (schools and colleges) with different governing entities, organizational rules and processes, as well as unique traditions.

The key is to plan jointly. Skipping this single step can have disastrous consequences. Joint planning provides time to understand challenges at the different institutions in order to make decisions that are equitable. It also serves to provide partners with control over decisions that are made and, therefore, earn "buy-in" for the plan. People who have a say in the decisions made that affect them are more likely to be satisfied in the partnership.[3]

## AVOID A "COOKIE-CUTTER" APPROACH

You are likely to find in early strategic planning sessions that a "cookie-cutter" approach does not work. What works in one region does not necessarily work in another; what works in one school in one district might not be well-received in another. Additionally, you should find that a mandate from the top is a potential barrier to success. The challenge is to achieve your STEM goals while working with partners that have unique cultures.

As long as core partners (K–12 teachers and administrators and university science and mathematics and science and mathematics education faculty) are at the table in each regional and state-level partnership, it is okay for each region to organize differently, given their cultural uniqueness. Partnerships in your state may be sprawled across the state, and vary significantly in numbers and in size. The term "partner" is applicable whether you are using it to include the governing body of your state university system; institutions of higher education, from Research I universities to small, regional universities; the state department of education; classroom teachers in a rural school; the largest urban school district in your state; or two-year community colleges.

The key is for state, regional, and local partnerships to all work in tandem, with structures that are transparent, so that all parties are able to see the work at all levels and to keep all pieces coherent and focused on the agenda of improving student achievement in science and mathematics, kindergarten through college.

Listening and learning about each other at face-to-face meetings helps all members of your partnership feel they were being treated fairly. Another strategy for success is to find similarities, form connections, and then build on them. Still another is to celebrate the differences.

If your partnership needs to take time to plan jointly and allows flexibility in how each partner accomplishes success in reaching common partnership goals, then you should find that it is important to include time on each monthly meeting agenda of your STEM leadership team to discuss changes in strategy. Have partners share information about how and why they adapted strategies to attain the common goals. Due to these adaptations and adjustments to the implementation plan, an important role for your state leadership team is to monitor progress to ensure alignment at the local and regional levels to the overall goals, to ensure common understanding, to guide decision-making, as well as to determine whether the overall implementation plan needs adjustment. You are likely to find that time for joint planning and sharing is another key strategy to reaching goals of improved student success.

## Involve Key People in the Work

To begin building a foundation for change to improve students' success in science and mathematics, people may be invited to participate who are already overburdened with the duties of their regular jobs. In addition, education reform is both so prevalent and so hard to implement that most educators would rather run the other way than voluntarily participate. Difficulties in the change process are usually perceived as mismanagement rather than a normal condition of changing practice (DuFour and Eaker 1998, 48).

Recommendations for engaging in reform have sometimes been fraught with admonitions to avoid conflict or to smooth over problems that actually impede progress. Once key stakeholders have agreed to become involved, partnership development priorities include developing ownership and responsibility, and involving administrators who support the work.

You may find that some key individuals that you would like to involve in your STEM partnership have reservations about the amount of extra work entailed. Some potential partners may not want to participate because they want to avoid needless controversy. These two examples are intended to offer an important lesson about partnerships: If you want people to participate, it is absolutely critical for all members to gain something from the partnership; otherwise key people are likely say no to your invitation to participate.

When determining whom to invite, four solutions are found to be effective: (1) involve both school and college administrators (e.g. principals, provosts); (2) develop common goals that allow the work to be completed within the parameters of educators' approved work and existing structures; (3) provide extra compensation; and (4) appeal to altruism.

***Example: PRISM Region Involvement of Key People.*** In one PRISM region, major stakeholders capitalized on a set of common goals. Activities were developed to meet current and critical needs of teachers and higher education faculty, not just extra work that was added onto already busy schedules. Partners' roles were well-defined across activities and projects. University faculty members' contributions were based on providing content expertise and K–12 teachers and coordinators brought their understanding of teachers' and students' needs to the partnership. Teachers appreciated the professional learning they experienced to the extent that they developed a presentation for their principal describing the merits and accomplishment of their PRISM work.

## BREAK DOWN CULTURAL BARRIERS: FINDING COMMON GROUND

Regardless of previous experience in partnerships or collaboratives, each partner maintains his or her own unique work culture. Large cultural differences exist between higher education faculty and K–12 teachers, but differences also exist between school districts, and even between schools. However, the K–12 and university cultures could not be further apart organizationally and legislatively.

For instance, K–12 school accountability horrifies higher education faculty. Likewise, a class of 300 students (common on college campuses) petrifies teachers. Clashes need not be predictable. Partners need only to come to respect each other's culture, even if they cannot understand it, by being open, listening, and asking questions. Joint leadership, with representation from key stakeholder groups, provides positive role models and contributes to the atmosphere of trust.

It is important for partnership meetings to become neutral "spaces" for cultures to connect and for people to learn from one another in a nonthreatening environment. Opportunities are needed in initial meetings for people to learn about each other's culture. Breakthroughs become possible when leaders patiently facilitate the dialog between higher education faculty and public school teachers. Examples of success include: (1) asking questions to try to understand cultural issues; (2) visiting each other's classrooms; (3) initiating offers to collaborate; and (4) making changes in one's own instructional practices.

### Watch Out When Expanding Traditional Roles

Selecting a K–16 approach to respond to the STEM challenge may seem logical, but when creating new projects to improve science and mathematics student achievement, teachers and university faculty can be illogically placed in roles that are unclear, unfamiliar, or sometimes uncomfortable. Educators may be asked to assume roles for which they have no informal or formal training. Nontraditional roles can be made more bearable if training is provided and clear definitions of roles are developed.

## K–16 Educators as Co-learners

Since the goal is to improve science and mathematics student achievement in both schools and colleges, a useful strategy (that also helps to strengthen K–16 partnerships) is the creation of K–16 learning communities as a professional learning model (see chapter 6). In order to implement these learning communities comprised of higher education faculty and K–12 teachers, higher education faculty have to assume new roles as collegial learners, as well as provide professional development. Teachers have a reciprocal role of teaching pedagogical knowledge and assessment strategies to their higher education STEM faculty colleagues. For K–16 STEM professional learning communities to be effective, it is important to help all partners feel comfortable in these nontraditional roles. One way to accomplish this is to develop "definition documents" that clearly define roles and responsibilities, as well as describe concepts and new organizational structures. (See section below on *PRISM Definition Documents.*)

Training may also be useful in a variety of formats to suit different needs. For example, one PRISM region hosted an action research conference for higher education faculty; another worked with small groups of faculty and teachers on characteristics of successful professional learning communities; a third region worked one-on-one with higher education faculty to provide new skills in facilitation and collaboration. Again, it is important to use state and regional leadership team meetings as friendly territory where K–16 educators can learn to work together comfortably as they gain the knowledge and skills to successfully grow into their new nontraditional roles.

*Example: PRISM Collaborators.*    One of the earliest goals in one PRISM region was to nurture K–16 relationships to form collaborative groups. PRISM brought together the support of its resources, the encouragement of its leaders, and a vision of regional collaboration, all of which helped to cultivate closer working relationships. The partnership grew as a result of the support, but it also deepened because of the importance of the PRISM goals.

Most participants in this region stated that the single most important result from PRISM was that of the partnerships established among K–12 teachers and higher education faculty. Learning communities became the primary vehicle for teacher professional learning. K–12 teachers stated that the greatest benefits of their partnerships with higher education faculty were collegial learning and enhanced content knowledge.

## SHARE COMMON GOALS

A critical factor in sustaining a partnership is to develop common goals toward which to work. Finding common goals helps individuals identify with the STEM reform initiative, as well as help meet individual goals. Kingsley and Waschak (2005) explain that the value added in working collaboratively is to find common goals. Therefore, start at the earliest stages and jointly develop common goals for the project. Continue to monitor common understandings and progress toward common goals throughout as formative assessment.

It is important for partners to determine a limited number of goals that define the direction of the work, especially encompassing both K–12 and higher education issues (Gomez et al. 1990). For example, a STEM initiative in your state likely has the shared goals of enhancing student learning and developing better teachers. Within these broad goals, you find it helpful for your state leadership team to engage in frequent discussions in order to come to consensus on defining the essential elements of the scope of work of your partnership. You find an overall goal of improving science and mathematics student learning to be compelling. It likely fits into school improvement plans, higher education frameworks for learning, and parental desires for their children.

## BUILD IN FLEXIBILITY

Winkler and Fretchling (2005) divide obligations into two types: operational and intellectual. To paraphrase, partners need to find a balance between their career responsibilities and their partnership obligations, including challenges such as increased workload associated with partnership work. It is important to find a balance between creating mutual needs, promoting a sense of community through the partnership, and remembering that all partners have primary accountability to their employers, as well as a desire to achieve their own individual goals.

One helpful hint is to align goals *and* create an individualized approach to meeting them. You are likely to find that this flexible way of achieving common goals becomes the "glue" that keeps your partnership together. Each institution and school district partner must assess its own needs and then tackle its own issues to achieve the common goals. A flexible model of achieving common goals necessitates the development of concentric leadership levels to constantly monitor the work. The participation of the state-level project director in every regional meeting is a good trade-off for it leads to high-level participation and to solid results.

*Example: PRISM Flexibility.* In PRISM, building in flexibility to achieve common goals brought with it a slight risk. Schools could opt-out. Additionally, regions or teams within regions could move away from the common goals to work on their own agendas, perhaps without implicit knowledge of doing so, and jeopardize the outcomes. At the beginning of PRISM, one school district chose not to participate because of the open-ended feeling of not having a predictable structure of activities. Their departure provided room for three additional school districts eager to "sign on" as partners.

## MEASURE PROGRESS: USING DATA-DRIVEN DECISION-MAKING

Using data to assess one's needs is the essence of changing practice, from the classroom to the state level. A data-driven approach is needed to determine whether your partnership is on track and your decision-making on target. Assigning an evaluator to the leadership team is critical to ensure that your STEM reform work is evaluated, and benchmarks and outcomes are monitored. You also find an evaluator helpful when assessing the growth of your STEM partnership. An evaluator can recommend existing assessment tools related to measuring progress of partnerships or help the team develop new ones.

Although it may be time-consuming, please consider having the leadership team develop its own partnership assessment tools. Such an activity creates an opportunity for intellectual dialog that can be value added. Developing your own indicators of evidence and coming to consensus on the definition of success helps your partners better understand the vision and common goals. Your partnership can benefit from developing its own assessment tools, but can use the ones described below as a point of departure.

## TOOLS DEVELOPED IN PRISM

The PRISM state leadership team followed a design-implementation-outcomes (DIO) process improvement cycle (Callow-Heuser et al. 2005) to refine interventions and strategies. It also developed a set of tools to monitor the soundness of the partnership as well as to measure its progress toward project goals (See chapter 8 for more information on evaluating large-scale projects.) Measurement tools that were developed included: (1) a partnership rubric, (2) definition documents, and (3) a set of management tools. These tools helped to accelerate and expand awareness and understanding of project goals and to attend consciously to the deepening of the partnership.

*PRISM Partnership Rubric.* Through numerous conversations and several working drafts, the PRISM state leadership team developed a partnership rubric. Indicators believed to be the most important to forming and sustaining PRISM partnerships were based on the literature at the time and included: "vision and goals," "communication," "decision making," "responsibility and accountability," and "change and sustainability." The indicators formed strands that described different stages of partnership growth ("beginning," "emerging," "developing," and "accomplished").

The use of this rubric did not result in one correct answer nor did it produce a rating or score; rather, the outcome portrayed a snapshot of strengths and weaknesses that each partnership could use to guide progress over time. Using consensus-based decision-making, reasoning had to be articulated when marking one indicator level or another. Through discussion, misconceptions were cleared up and the group formed a common understanding of what an accomplished PRISM partnership should be. These useful discussions defining the vision of PRISM partnerships were carried to the regions and shared among the various partners. The rubric was used for formative assessment and planning purposes at all levels. See appendix 2.1 for a copy of the PRISM partnership rubric.

*PRISM Definition Documents.* Experts in evaluating partnerships suggest that indicators such as having a shared vision and common goals are critical to the success of a partnership (Winkler and Fretchling 2005). PRISM definition documents were created to characterize new PRISM organizational ideas so that all partners would understand and share the vision. Writing down the characteristics of a learning community or the definition of a Regional Coordinating Committee helped partners form the same vision. The ultimate goal was to encourage partners to change culture and practices. These documents were posted on PRISM's website and distributed where appropriate. See appendix 2.2 for a sample of a definition document.

*PRISM Management Tools.* Coburn (2003) suggests that to bring a reform initiative to scale, four interrelated dimensions need to be addressed: depth, sustainability, spread, and shift in ownership. PRISM used its partnership in a management capacity to ensure that the work was brought to scale. Management tools were developed as a way to guide decision-making in bringing PRISM to scale, and also to actualize the Math and Science Partnership Program (MSP) 5 Key Features.

The five key features (partnership-driven; teacher quality, quantity, and diversity; challenging courses and curriculum; evidence-based design and outcomes; and institutional change and sustainability) are integrated goals to which all MSP grants must contribute. PRISM strategies were mapped onto the key features to create a set of assessments from which to monitor progress. Defining questions guided raters to provide evidence for dimensions such as depth, sustainability, spread, and shift in ownership that would capture changes in practices and lead to institutionalization.

On an annual basis, the state leadership team rated itself on features and dimensions that comprised the section on the MSP key feature, partnership-driven. Each region completed its regional section, as well. Ratings started with "no progress" and moved to "sustained" across scales that measured a practice from "emerging" to "change institutionalized." Results were used by the state and regions to determine where progress was being made and sustained, as well as where additional emphasis needed to be placed in order to achieve PRISM goals.

An analysis of the combined ratings for four years of the grant (ratings did not begin until year two), demonstrated a substantial decrease each year in the "no-progress" rating, with increases in the "sustained" rating (see figure 2.2). The partnership has been able to clearly define their roles and responsibilities in order to make hard decisions when needed.

The partnership has been able to support the work of all PRISM partners sharing progress on PRISM goals periodically to the Georgia Department of Education and University System of Georgia, as well through regional and local entities. Partners continue to experiment with ways to redirect non-NSF resources towards PRISM efforts and goals. The management tools are on pages fourteen to twenty-six of www.gaprism.org/presentations/reports/2008/tools_manage_projects.pdf.

## PRINCIPLES AND ACTION STEPS THAT LEAD TO SUCCESSFUL PARTNERSHIPS

Based on lessons learned through PRISM, a blueprint for healthy partnerships stems from an initial commitment of its members to hold one another accountable for contributions to common goals. Early partnership

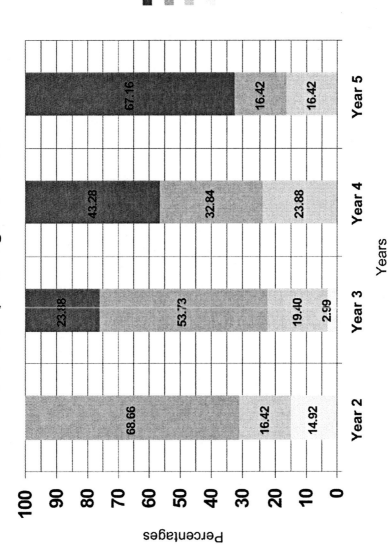

Figure 2.2. Results of Partnership-Driven Section of PRISM Management Tools

development must focus on clarifying roles and responsibilities and learning to work collaboratively. As the partnership matures, emphasis can be placed on sustaining the beliefs and practices that are found to be worthwhile in order to bring the reform efforts to scale. Five principles with a list of action steps are offered to guide development of a successful partnership in your state or region.

*Principle 1: Partnerships Require Continuous Attention.*   A key to success is a decision of your core leadership team to invest the necessary time and resources toward a continual process of partnership development, including training and ongoing assessment.

- Establish a regular meeting schedule
- Meet in a neutral site
- Build understanding of and experience in collaboration through training on partnership development
- Monitor implementation plans regularly
- Hold retreats for long-term planning

*Principle 2: Leadership Must Be Shared.*   Create a shared model of leadership among the public schools and higher education, at local and regional levels, and between state departments of education and university systems at the state level. A representative sample of responsible parties should lead by example to encourage members to become jointly responsible for the work. The three-way collaboration of arts and sciences faculty, education faculty, and K–12 teachers is a critical cornerstone to success.

- Break down cultural barriers
- Plan everything jointly
- Involve key people in the work

*Principle 3: Partners Must Be Given Flexibility to Accomplish Project Goals.*   Your partnership must be designed so that members collaborate on common goals. However, to capitalize on unique contextual and cultural differences, it is important to provide flexibility on how to meet project goals so that partners can concurrently work toward individual goals.

- Avoid the "cookie cutter" approach—allow for differences among partners
- Keep your partnership structure transparent
- Share common goals

***Principle 4: Decisions Must Be Data-Driven.***   At all levels, it is important for STEM partnerships to use a process of ongoing formative assessment to improve their partnerships. A variety of measurement tools are needed and used to evaluate your partnerships' attributes, as real, sustainable change develops.

- When tools are needed and don't exist—create them yourself
- Include representatives of the evaluation team in your leadership team

***Principle 5: Communication Is Critical.***   Collaboration is built on good communication. Partnerships must include overlapping levels of leadership to build consensus and to foster understanding. Communication is ensured if partners work as equals and develop trust in and respect for each other.

- Establish an avenue or mechanism for communicating with all partners
- Listen and be open to exploring new ideas
- Take the necessary time to build trust
- Take time to learn each other's culture and learn from one another

## NOTES

1. Nancy Vandergrift is a regional program coordinator in the Partnership for Reform In Science and Mathematics (PRISM), a systemic K–16 STEM initiative in Georgia. She is also a program coordinator for the College of Education at the University of Georgia. Sheila Jones is the project director of PRISM. She taught high school mathematics and is the senior executive director for P–16 Programs for the University System of Georgia.

2. See Introduction, chapter 1.

3. See chapter 5 for an excellent example of a top-down decision concerning professional development made without the support or knowledge of the partnership.

**3**

# CONNECTING A K–16 STEM INITIATIVE TO STATE SCIENCE AND MATHEMATICS CURRICULUM

*Amy S. Mast*[1]

## INTRODUCTION

**A**s teachers, administrators, business leaders, parents, and policy makers in every state know, a key element of increasing student achievement in science and mathematics is providing all students with access to a rigorous curriculum. The Education Trust (2000) has been sending the message for years that the completion of challenging courses is one of the most important leverage points for increasing student achievement. Since establishing science and mathematics curricula is the responsibility of states, how do those who are committed to a Science, Technology, Engineering, and Mathematics (STEM) K–16 initiative promote curricular change and connect with the state's efforts in curriculum?

This chapter has two purposes. It describes how to engage education policy makers, K–12 educators, and college faculty in changing a state's K–12 curriculum in science and mathematics. It also describes how to connect a STEM K–16 initiative to a state's efforts to change its curriculum. Successful examples are shared from actual participant experience in developing and implementing a more rigorous K–12 curriculum in Georgia, called the Georgia Performance Standards (GPS), and from Georgia's STEM Initiative, called the Partnership for Reform In Science and Mathematics (PRISM).

How to develop statewide training, curricular frameworks, instructional strategies, teacher resources, and how to build public support are emphasized. How to capitalize on the unique role and involvement of higher education faculty at every level of curricular development and implementation, as well as their involvement in training current teachers to teach in a standards-based classroom, are discussed. Strategies are described on how to incorporate a state's new curriculum and more effective modes of instructional practices into university teacher-preparation programs. Finally, how a state can change its high school graduation requirements to include four years of mathematics and four years of science courses is described. The chapter closes with a summary of action steps.

## PURPOSE OF A STATE CURRICULUM

Although the language varies from state to state, typically a state curriculum specifies standards—or what students are expected to know in each subject and grade. Generally these are minimum standards, allowing local school districts to exceed them. The state's curriculum generally serves as a guideline for instruction that helps teachers, students, and parents know what topics must be covered and mastered in particular courses.

A state's accountability system then includes a combination of tests that are aligned to the curricular standards. Again, there are variations among states, but typically students are required to get passing scores on some of these tests to progress from grade to grade and to fulfill part of the requirements for high school graduation.

## HIGHLIGHTING NEED FOR A NEW STATE CURRICULUM IN SCIENCE AND MATHEMATICS

A key first step to increasing the rigor of a state curriculum in science and mathematics is to have an outside, independent organization conduct an external curriculum audit and disseminate the findings to the public. In Georgia's case, the State Board of Education commissioned Phi Delta Kappa International (2002) to conduct a curriculum audit of Georgia's K–12 curriculum in the fall of 2001. Georgia's curriculum had also been reviewed and given a grade B in mathematics and an F in science by the Thomas B. Fordham Institute (2000) in its *State of the State Standards, 2000* report card.

The findings and recommendations from these external reviews helped draw attention to the need for dramatic change in the state's K–12 curriculum in science and mathematics. The external reviews helped galvanize policy makers, educators, business leaders, and key education partners to highlight to the public why the state's curriculum in science and mathematics needed to change.

## LEADING MONUMENTAL CHANGE WITH AUTHORITY AND RESOLVE

Reports can often times end up gathering dust on bookshelves, even well-written reports from external experts that contain alarming findings. Unless people with leadership and authority leverage the findings and recommendations into action, the bookshelf is often a report's final resting place. Strong and steadfast leadership is a key component in embarking on strengthening a state's curriculum.

In 2001, members of the Georgia State Board of Education, the Governor, and several other state education officials were instrumental in initiating a review of the state's curriculum. A new State Superintendent of Schools was elected in Georgia in 2002. With the support of the State Board of Education and under the leadership of a new State Superintendent of Schools, the Georgia Department of Education began the process of redeveloping the state's K–12 curriculum, using the findings and recommendations in the Phi Delta Kappa audit report. Having strong commitment and leadership from both the State Board of Education and the State Superintendent to guide such a large-scale curriculum change was an essential and necessary component for Georgia.

***Example: Georgia Curriculum Leadership Revision.*** Superintendent Cox announced in early 2003 that the Georgia Department of Education would revise and strengthen the curriculum in all four core content areas (English and Language Arts, Social Studies, Science, and Mathematics) to accomplish the following:

Drive instruction and assessment
Provide guidelines for teachers, students, and test makers
Teach to a commonly held curriculum, not to tests or textbooks
Align state tests with established standards
Base standards on effective practices as in high-performing states

While each state's political context is different and transition a constant factor, it is essential to have leaders that can speak with conviction about why curriculum changes in science and mathematics need to be made in order to prepare students for college and work. When developing and implementing more rigorous curriculum standards, leaders are often confronted in the press and in public with resistance to such change. Local and state newspaper headlines often highlight the fears of the public about increasing rigor and the doubts about raising expectations for all students.

Leaders who take on the hard work of developing a more rigorous curriculum must stay the course during the challenging times of development, implementation, predictable dips in assessment scores, and calls to lower expectations and rigor. Leadership is a critical component when beginning a major change in curriculum, and leaders must have the authority and resolve not only to weather public doubt and criticism but also to effectively communicate the necessity to raise standards and expectations.

> We are beginning the most extensive improvement in Georgia education undertaken in the last 18 years—the implementation of the Georgia Performance Standards (GPS). The new state curriculum sets high standards, maintains clear expectations, and will place our schools and our students not just at the top of the Southeast, but at the top of the nation.[2]

## ESTABLISHING AUTHORITY FOR DECISION-MAKING BODIES

When embarking on statewide curricular change in science and mathematics, it may be useful to appoint Expert Advisory Panels in each of these fields and give them authority to determine a plan for curriculum development. Use of Expert Advisory Panels may help you avoid some conflicts or pitfalls that typically emerge when engaged in the development of new state curricular standards.

One approach is to charge each Expert Advisory Panel with finding the best available curriculum standards in the nation or in the world and then to use them to guide development of statewide performance standards. Such Expert Advisory Panels could be asked to determine basic tenets and principles so that curriculum teams could begin their writing with a shared set of goals and beliefs.

In Georgia, Expert Advisory Panels were used. The panel chose the Japanese Mathematics Standards (Japan Ministry of Education, Science, and Culture, 1989) to shape and guide the development of the high school mathematics curriculum, and felt these lean, coherent, rigorous, and clear standards would best meet the needs of Georgia students. They also chose to use the North Carolina Mathematics Standards (2003) as a model format for readability, clarity, and organization. A separate panel agreed to base the new science curriculum on the *Benchmarks for Scientific Literacy* by the American Association for the Advancement of Science (1993) with alignment to the *National Science Education Standards* from the National Research Council (1996).

## FORMING CURRICULUM WRITING TEAMS

Once a direction had been agreed upon, curricular writing teams were formed in Georgia, initially consisting of teachers and mathematics and science supervisors. The curriculum writing teams were charged with developing content standards that were performance based. They were to consist of content and process standards, sample tasks, student work, and teacher commentary.

When completed, the new Georgia curricular standards were sent out for public comment—including to the University System of Georgia (a state public higher education system of thirty-five colleges and universities). The Academic Advisory Committees in mathematics and in the sciences within the University System of Georgia were specifically asked to give feedback.

### Mathematics Feedback from the University System of Georgia (USG)

The Advisory Committee on Mathematical Subjects (ACMS) raised serious concerns about the proposed mathematics curriculum standards. Their commentary stated that as mathematicians and mathematics educators representing USG institutions, they had serious doubts about the proposed curriculum because of problems in the mathematics content and concerns about the proposed implementation timeline and plan. The committee provided examples of specific mathematics content concepts, topics, and tasks that needed to be corrected.

The ACMS concluded their detailed feedback report by stating that the curriculum revision process had so far adopted an approach in which college faculty were merely informed of the proposed curriculum standards that were to prepare students for college and only later asked for their feedback. They recommended a more open and collaborative process of engaging and involving faculty in the curriculum's development.

The ACMS asked for closer cooperation with the Department of Education. They expressed their deep interest and commitment in working more collaboratively on helping to develop and improve the curriculum, providing better coordination between teacher education programs and expectations for new teachers that would serve in K–12 schools, and facilitating deeper involvement of USG mathematics faculty in development activities for in-service teachers.

The Georgia Department of Education issued a press release expressing the desire to be inclusive and open in welcoming and receiving feedback from university professors. Much of the feedback from the USG Academic Committees was used to improve the proposed curriculum. Higher education mathematics faculty members were invited to participate as colleagues with the Georgia Department of Education in the redesign of the K–12 mathematics curriculum. When the new mathematics curriculum was presented to the State Board of Education for approval, it was fully embraced by the higher education mathematics community.

*Example: Statement of the Mathematics Advisory Committee, USG— Presented to State Board of Education, May 12, 2005.* The knowledge and skills that a Georgia high school graduate needs to be successful in college, in the military, or on entry into a high-tech economy require access to the same rigorous curriculum.

Jobs that are characterized as routine in nature, do not involve significant problem solving, and do not involve creativity are jobs that are now being outsourced and continue to be subject to outsourcing to other countries or to be filled by unskilled labor. Consequently, Georgia students finishing high school need to take responsibility for their own learning, be lifelong learners, be creative, be problem solvers, be adaptable, and have a strong background in mathematics, science, and technology.

Georgia has adapted from the Japanese mathematics curriculum the following characteristics:

1. fewer topics at each grade level
2. more rigor and depth
3. an integrated curriculum
4. a clear, focused path to higher (college) mathematics

The Georgia Performance Standards for mathematics are characterized by the four R's:

1. Rigor
2. Relevance
3. Relationships, and
4. Reasoning

The Standards strike a balance between concepts, skills, and problem solving. The curriculum provides more depth in concepts than its predecessor, presents real and relevant tasks, and remains strong in computational skills. The Standards offer three sequences (core, regular, and accelerated) that require students to attain a common level of mastery and allow students to move from one sequence to another upon completion of periodic benchmarks.

The Standards require the mastery of the skills, fluency, understanding, and experience needed for economic success regardless of a student's potential choice of vocation or career. Specifically, they provide a path that enables any student to achieve excellence in careers that demand a high level of mathematical ability.

This revision of the high school GPS resulted from collaboration by master classroom teachers, district- and regional-level mathematics leadership, and higher education faculty from both mathematical science departments and colleges of education.

The committee is proud to present the proposed high school Georgia Performance Standards for adoption.

## Lesson Learned

It is clear from Georgia's experience that K–16 teams of educators need to be involved in writing curriculum in science and mathematics. It is not an endeavor, especially at the scale of a statewide curriculum overhaul, that can be accomplished by individuals working alone, or only by K–12 educators, or only by higher education faculty working in isolation.

When a state board of education, state school superintendent, and the state education agency initiate a change in the curricular standards, requesting review and feedback from the higher education community is not enough. Full partnership, involvement, and engagement of higher education faculty need to occur from the beginning of curriculum development.

From experience in Georgia, we know that many faculty members want to be involved in helping improve K–12 curriculum and want to be a part of working with K–12 teachers more directly. Their high levels of involvement in the final version of the science and mathematics curriculum can help gain public support for the new curriculum. In turn, faculty participation in curriculum development can help higher education institutions become aware of the need to change teacher preparation programs so that new teachers are able to teach the new K–12 curriculum.

## MAXIMIZING PARTNERSHIP OPPORTUNITIES

It is important for K–16 STEM initiatives to connect with a state's efforts to raise or change curricular standards in science and mathematics. Georgia's STEM initiative, called the Partnership for Reform In Science and Mathematics (PRISM) began after the curriculum revision in Georgia had begun. One strategy within PRISM was to raise and align science and mathematics student-learning standards and curriculum. PRISM was able to play a key role in Georgia in supporting the development of the science and mathematics curriculum, professional learning of teachers, and implementation of the Georgia Performance Standards.

Through the K–16 STEM initiative in your state, it should be possible to bring college and university faculty to the table to collaborate with your State School Superintendent's efforts to strengthen curriculum in science and mathematics. It is important to ensure the participation of higher education science and mathematics faculty at every step of the curriculum development and implementation process.

It is also important to include senior-level staff from your state education agency on the state-level leadership team in your STEM initiative. In this way your state leadership team can facilitate communication and recruit higher education faculty members to serve on curriculum standards, curriculum tasks, and framework writing teams.

Funding, if available through your STEM initiative, can help your state education agency to develop additional curricular resources, tools, materials, videos, and web casts to improve teacher content knowledge and instructional strategies in science and mathematics. You could provide science and mathematics teachers with professional learning opportunities to enable greater teacher readiness for implementation of the state curricular standards.

## ENLISTING AND PUBLICIZING FOLLOW-UP
## EXTERNAL REVIEWS AND AUDITS

Following development and approval of new curricular standards in science and mathematics, it is important to have outside experts conduct follow-up reviews and audits to find out what improvements a state has made. Such reviews can provide a state with feedback, benchmarking and tracking the state's progress in designing a standards- and performance-based curriculum that prepares students for college and work. Having outside and independent reviews and audits are especially important in building public trust and confidence in the quality of content standards and curriculum.

For example, in Georgia, the new science curriculum was reviewed in 2005, and given a grade of B and placed on the national honor roll of state's curriculum by the Thomas B. Fordham Institute (2005). The report said that "Georgia had the 'most improved' science standards in the nation, a vast improvement from the grade of F that the state's science standards received in 2000." Georgia's K–8 new mathematics standards and the 1998 mathematics high school standards were reviewed, and given a grade of B and placed on the national honor roll of state curricula. The high school mathematics curriculum was scheduled to be reviewed and adopted by the State Board of Education later that year.

Unfortunately, some people have expressed concern about whether all students have the ability to succeed in a more rigorous curriculum, particularly in the areas of science and math. However, it is interesting to note that in high schools where requirements have been strengthened, students can and do learn at higher levels when challenged to do so. Equally important, by raising the curriculum standards, these schools have given their students more choices and opportunities for successful careers in the growing fields of science, math, engineering and technology.[3]

## BENCHMARKING AND ALIGNING TO REPUTABLE
## NATIONAL AND INTERNATIONAL STANDARDS

### Mathematics Standards

When a state's standards are benchmarked against national and international standards, such as the National Council of Teachers of Mathematics (1989) and College Board (2007), they are likely to be more rigorous, include fewer topics at every grade level, include a strong data analysis strand, and feature integrated high school courses. The curriculum is more likely to stress a balance of concepts, skills, and problem solving emphasizing relevance and real-world contexts.

## Science Standards

When the *Benchmarks for Science Literacy* (American Association for the Advancement of Science 1993) and the National Research Council's (1996) *National Science Education Standards* are used as the benchmark, K–12 science standards are more likely to provide students with knowledge and skills for proficiency in science. They are also more likely to emphasize the process and nature of science as well as content to encourage inquiry-based instruction. Finally, greater progress is likely for students to actually "do" science at every grade level and not just "view" science. Hands-on, student-centered, and inquiry-based approaches are emphasized.

## STAGGERING AND PHASING-IN IMPLEMENTATION

Asking teachers, particularly K–8 teachers, to implement new standards in multiple content areas in a single year is not reasonable. The development of a sound plan for the roll-out of the new standards is crucial to both student learning and teacher buy-in. A phased-in approach can help elementary teachers not have to learn, teach, and implement new curriculum standards in every subject for every grade.

## REVISING, IMPROVING, AND RETOOLING TRAINING AND PROFESSIONAL LEARNING

With state board adoption of new curricular standards in science and mathematics, typically state education agencies design and deliver massive statewide training for teachers, curriculum directors, and administrators. One approach is to begin the training the year before teachers are to implement the curriculum in the classroom. Another approach is to use a "Train-the-Trainer" model or have teams of teachers from the same school attend training together. Revisions to training can be made by using feedback from participant surveys to better meet the needs of teachers.

## DEVELOPING TEACHER TASKS, FRAMEWORKS, RESOURCES, AND TOOLS FOR TEACHERS

In an effort to provide teachers with the tasks, student work, and commentary intended to illustrate new state standards, instructional frameworks are needed at every grade level. Here is another way the K–16 STEM initiative in your state can connect with the curricular work of your state education agency. Your STEM initiative can include, as an important strategy, the development of instructional frameworks that are created by collaborative teams of K–12 teachers and higher education faculty. These K–16 science and mathematics teams are able to provide educators with a curriculum map and instructional units. Each unit contains the key standards addressed, enduring understandings, essential questions, sequential real-world tasks, and a culminating task.

Through the K–16 STEM initiative in your state, when partnering with your state education agency, instructional tools can be developed for teachers to use to implement any new state standards. A centralized Web site can be created for the instructional frameworks containing content and process standards, tasks, student work, teacher commentary, videos of classrooms in which the standards are being taught, web casts that provide content resources for middle school teachers, parent letters, and concept maps.

## PROFESSIONAL LEARNING FOR PROFESSIONAL DEVELOPMENT PROVIDERS

Another way your K–16 STEM initiative can connect to the work of your state education agency is in providing professional learning for the professional developers in your state. In Georgia many professional developers are science and mathematics specialists at Regional Education Service Agencies (RESAs). Through your K–16 STEM initiative, a useful strategy is to bring department of education content specialists and higher education faculty members into partnership with the professional developers in your state to design professional learning for science and mathematics teachers who are the implementers of the new state standards (see examples in chapter 5).

## COLLABORATING WITH UNIVERSITY TEACHER PREPARATION PROGRAMS

In order to implement new curriculum standards in K–12 schools, teachers must be prepared with content knowledge and instructional strategies to teach the students. As discussed, it is critically important for the K–12 community to reach out and fully involve higher education partners in developing and implementing K–12 curriculum. In preparing the teaching workforce to teach new curriculum standards, it is just as important for higher education institutions to fully partner with the K–12 community in order to integrate the K–12 curriculum into their programs of study. The K–16 STEM initiative in your state can help to solidify such partnerships.

When a state is implementing new curricular standards in science and mathematics, a gap is likely to appear between the new standards and teacher candidates completing teacher preparation programs that same year. One strategy to consider within your K–16 STEM initiative is development of a New Teacher Symposium for Science and Mathematics. The Symposium can be designed to provide professional learning to new teachers who did not receive exposure to the state's new K–12 curriculum standards within their teacher preparation programs and to teachers who have moved in from another state.

Another strategy that can be included in your K–16 STEM initiative is to support and conduct professional learning on the state's new curriculum for higher education faculty members from colleges of arts and sciences and education who collaboratively prepare the next generations of science and mathematics teachers. Each session can be co-planned and co-led by one K–12 facilitator and one higher education faculty member.

In order for teachers to be prepared for teaching new curriculum standards, it is critical that partnerships are formed between higher education institutions and the K–12 community. It is also necessary for all curriculum materials and resources to be accessible and used by higher education faculty in teacher preparation programs. An example of how to do this can be found in chapter 7.

## CHANGING A STATE'S HIGH SCHOOL GRADUATION REQUIREMENTS

A useful partner in your K–16 STEM initiative is the American Diploma Project, led by Achieve, Inc., if your state is a participant. The American Diploma Project (ADP) Network (2005) includes states committed to raising expectations and achievement in American high schools so that students graduate with the knowledge and skills they need to be successful in college and the workplace and that many more students succeed in college once enrolled.

I applaud the recent action by the State Board of Education to raise high school graduation requirements and to establish a solid academic core of courses for all students so that all will be prepared for post-secondary education or for more complex entry level jobs in the workforce.

It is very important that the new high school graduation requirements align with the expectations and competencies needed in postsecondary education and work. To this end, state education agencies and the business community have supported the Department of Education's efforts and are now working collaboratively to ensure that the necessary alignments and expectations are in place.[4]

Joining the ADP Network can be a critical component to begin the process of a state board of education requiring more science and mathematics courses for high school graduation.

In Georgia, through a partnership of the State Department of Education, the University System of Georgia and other post-secondary institutions, and PRISM, it has been possible to change the curricular requirements for high school graduation in science and mathematics and to align them with college admission requirements.

Georgia's two-tiered diploma, where students followed either College Preparatory or Technology and Career coursework, has been eliminated. Under the new rule, all students are expected to complete a common set of requirements to earn a regular high school diploma, including four years of science and four years of mathematics.

## RECOMMENDED ACTION STEPS

By way of summary, this chapter closes with a set of action steps that states can follow to both strengthen curriculum in science and mathematics and to position this work as a central component of K–16 STEM initiatives at state and local levels.

- Enlist external curriculum audits or reviews by an independent organization and publicize results to draw attention to the need for curricular change.
- Have strong commitment and resolve from key policy makers with the authority to lead raising standards and expectations.
- Establish expert advisory panels with authority to review curriculum standards from other states, countries, and groups, and create a plan for developing new curriculum standards.

- Create curriculum writing teams to develop performance-based content standards.
- Solicit and respond to feedback on proposed curriculum drafts from teachers, higher education faculty, and the public.
- Connect STEM initiatives to a state's efforts to raise curricular standards in mathematics and science.
- Facilitate collaboration between college and university faculty and K–12 leaders and educators in all stages of curriculum development.
- Enlist follow-up external audits and reviews of new curricular standards to build public trust and confidence in their quality.
- Align and benchmark standards to national and international standards that are reputable, rigorous and balanced.
- Develop a reasonable plan to implement new standards to best promote student learning and teacher support, and deliver training that is reviewed to meet the needs of teachers.
- Develop instructional frameworks and tools for teachers that are created collaboratively by K–12 teachers and higher education faculty.
- Provide professional learning on new curriculum standards to the providers of professional development within your state.
- Collaborate with teacher-preparation programs to ensure that new teachers are prepared with content knowledge and instructional strategies to teach the new curriculum.
- Partner with national initiatives like the American Diploma Project and include K–12 teachers and higher education faculty to change high school graduation requirements and better prepare students for college and work.

## NOTES

1. Amy S. Mast is the associate director for K–12 in the Partnership for Reform In Science and Mathematics (PRISM), a systemic K–16 STEM initiative in Georgia. She is an education policy specialist and the director of implementation for Georgia's Alliance of Education Agency heads.
2. Kathy Cox, Georgia superintendent of schools.
3. Erroll Davis, chancellor of the University System of Georgia.
4. Erroll Davis, (2007), chancellor of the University System of Georgia.

**4**

# STUDENT INTEREST

## Choice and Achievement in Science and Mathematics

*Rosalind Barnes Fowler*[1]

## INTRODUCTION

**W**ith increasing evidence that the United States is losing ground in the areas of innovation, development, and the ability to compete globally in the new technology marketplace, there is a growing and pervasive need to draw immediate attention to this crisis.

One of the issues business leaders and educators cite as our most immediate concern is finding a solution to slowing our competitive decline and the growing gap in the number of skilled professionals working in the sciences, technology, engineering, and mathematics (STEM) as compared to the number of students who are pursuing or have expressed interest in these fields (Business Roundtable 2005; Committee on Prospering in the Global Economy of the 21st Century 2007).

Over the past decade, a great deal of attention has been given to enhancing curricular standards across the United States in efforts to improve student achievement in mathematics and science while also closing achievement gaps among demographic groups of student learners. Yet, as states and local governments have implemented models to improve curriculum and pedagogy as a means of enhancing student learning and achievement in the STEM fields, there is also a sense that efforts to decrease this competitive decline cannot rest solely on the shoulders of educators, business leaders, policy makers, or community activists.

Instead, with a closer examination of "who" these efforts are aimed to affect most—it seems only natural to begin recognizing an apparent lack of student interest and an increasing shift in student choice away from the STEM fields as one of the underlying concerns that school districts and communities must address if more immediate changes are to be accomplished.

The purpose of this chapter is give the reader a coherent set of strategies to increase student interest in science and mathematics—a necessary element of state and local efforts to increase student achievement in science and mathematics in American public schools. The suggested strategies are based on real experience in Georgia, learned through its Partnership for Reform In Science and Mathematics (PRISM).

## WHY STUDENT INTEREST IS IMPORTANT

Researchers have long linked students' prior knowledge and awareness of a particular subject to the improved learning as well as to improved interest in that subject. In their work, *The Strategic Teaching and Reading Project Guidebook*, Kujawa and Huske explain that "prior knowledge acts as a lens through which we view and absorb new information. It is a composite of who we are, based on what we have learned from both our academic and everyday experiences" (1995).

The more the link of the STEM fields to everyday life and experiences, the more likely it is that student interest can be piqued in the subject as being relevant and worthy of pursuing even in the face of difficulty. Of course, having this kind of interest—"well-developed individual interest" (Hidi and Renninger 2006)—encourages a student to attribute greater value to the subject, thus becoming curious, that drives additional knowledge gathering and increased persistence in the subject area despite looming obstacles or frustrations.

Additional research further contends that personal interest is a key factor behind youth's educational choice and career aspirations and that personal interest is often an indicator of student interest in scientific fields (Gardner, 1998). Gardner and Tamir (1989) explain that the term "interest" generally refers to a preference to engage in some types of activities rather than others. An interest may be regarded as a highly specific type of attitude: When interested in a particular phenomenon or activity, a person is more favorably inclined to attend to it and give time to it.

Most recently, ACT (2006) research supported the assertion that, at the very time our nation most needs promising students to enter STEM majors and careers, students' interest in these fields is on the decline. According to their "Developing the STEM Education Pipeline," over the past ten years, the percentage of ACT-tested students who said they were interested in majoring in engineering dropped steadily from 7.6 percent to 4.9 percent. Over the past five years, the percentage of ACT-tested students who said they were interested in majoring in computer and information science dropped steadily from 4.5 percent to 2.9 percent.

It stands to reason that if there is a link between student interest and improved learning, choices, and practices, then there needs to be ways to encourage student interest in the STEM fields as a means of increasing the number of students who decide to pursue these fields in college and in their careers.

## WHO INFLUENCES STUDENT INTEREST AND ACHIEVEMENT?

Numerous studies link teacher quality and effectiveness to student interest and achievement. In her study, "Teacher Quality and Student Achievement," Darling-Hammond (2000) stresses:

> Teachers' abilities to structure material, ask higher order questions, use student ideas, and probe student comments have also been found to be important variables in what students learn (Rosenshine and Furst 1973; Darling-Hammond et al. 1983; Good and Brophy 1986). No single instructional strategy has been found to be unvaryingly successful; instead, teachers who are able to use a broad repertoire of approaches skillfully (e.g., direct and indirect instruction, experience-based and skill-based approaches, lecture and small group work) are typically most successful. The use of different strategies occurs in the context of "active teaching" that is purposeful and diagnostic rather than random or laissez faire and that responds to students' needs as well as curriculum goals. (Good 1983)

When students are exposed to quality classroom teaching, their achievement in that subject soars. Compelling and consistent research over the past two decades points to the relevancy of quality classroom teachers with the appropriate content knowledge, experience, professional development, and general academic ability when seeking to promote student achievement more so than any other factor inside the classroom.

Perhaps the single most important driving force behind student achievement outside of the classroom is parental involvement. Recent studies concluded that student achievement improves when parents become involved in their children's education at school and in the community (Henderson and Mapp 2002). According to a three-year study of 12,000 students in nine high schools (Steinberg 1996), those school activities that draw parents into the schools physically (such as extracurricular activities, conferences, and "back to school" nights) are most effective in improving academic achievement. Researchers in this study concluded that "When parents come to school regularly, it reinforces the view in the child's mind that school and home are connected and that school is an integral part of the whole family's life."

## USING A PUBLIC AWARENESS CAMPAIGN TO SPARK STUDENT INTEREST

In Georgia, a public awareness campaign was included in its Partnership for Reform In Science and Mathematics (PRISM) that was funded by the National Science Foundation (NSF). This is the first time NSF provided support for such a campaign and their "eyes were on Georgia" to see if it would make a difference. NSF expected the principal investigator of PRISM to seek to gain valuable pre- and post-research to guide the development of the work and character of the collateral, messages, and eventual marketing of the effort.

With the agreement to use market research to shape and guide the development of the Public Awareness Campaign, the PRISM Initiative began the slow process of launching a campaign that would be deeply rooted in research and heavily scrutinized for theoretical soundness while also encouraging student interest in fields that strikes fear in most adults.

After participating in several rounds of respondent proposals to conduct market research in the state, one Boston-based agency surfaced with a company profile of strong ties to higher education and multidimensional research with children, adolescents and adult learners. Many respondents were more interested in providing all of the deliverables for the Public Awareness Campaign, focusing more on being principally involved in the final engagement of the target audience(s) and less concerned with becoming the independent organization that would help assess the effectiveness of the efforts.

What stood out most about the Massachusetts-based agency was that it focused heavily on making sure that our hypothesis and intention would be the right way to engage our audience. Their proposal suggested a timeline that would cover the full life of our NSF grant with three phases that would guide the development, measure message delivery, and then finally assess program effectiveness.

At the outset, there was a belief that the "student" would be the primary focus of the Public Awareness Campaign with smaller percentages of the attention devoted to the community at-large, parents, and educators. The team assembled to work with the market researchers spent time explaining their view of "how" the campaign would evolve over time and the role students would play.

Researchers were charged with helping form an understanding of the perception that students and various constituents had of the importance of student achievement in science and mathematics, what affected student interest and motivation to tackle rigorous coursework in those subjects, and what messages needed to be conveyed to the general public to encourage greater awareness of the importance of tackling mathematics and science education.

After talking with the Public Awareness Campaign director, the researchers determined that it would be necessary to talk to a number of people who influence or interact with students regularly, including the very students that are being targeted. Focus groups were held throughout the state with children ages six through fourteen; school counselors, teachers, principals, higher education faculty, community and business leaders; and PRISM leadership. Online, paper, and phone surveys were conducted with parents of school-aged children as well as ninth through eleventh grade high school students.

***Example: Campaign "Ah ha" Moment.***     During a focus group session with a group of fourth graders, one student explained how several weeks prior to our session she had math homework that she did not understand. So, as usual she went to her mom for help. She explained to the researchers that she and her mom completed her homework in no time, but when she turned in her work the following morning, the math answers were "all wrong." The young student said, without hesitation, "I'm never letting my mom help me with my homework again."

This innocent statement made us see for the first time the depth of the issues, perceptions, and concerns we would need to address in the Public Awareness Campaign if we wanted to encourage student achievement and interest in science and mathematics.

Taking approximately eight months to complete, the process of collecting qualitative and quantitative data, analyzing the data, and providing final recommendations was exhaustive and more time-consuming than the Public Awareness Campaign project director had originally imagined. The protracted process even caused angst among PRISM team members as many of the other aspects of the initiative were well in gear.

Once the final report was delivered, one astounding revelation was clear—students would not be the primary target audience. Instead, the student would be regarded as being a center of focus for engaging those who influence student behavior to encourage and support achievement in science and mathematics.

## HOW RESEARCH CAN HELP YOU SHAPE A PUBLIC AWARENESS CAMPAIGN IN YOUR STATE

If you make the same assumption that was made in Georgia, you may start with a model of treating a few constituents and audience members with the simple treatment and focus:

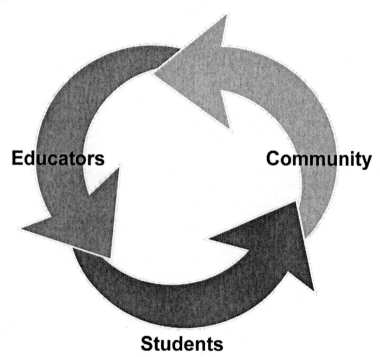

**Figure 4.1.   Model of treating a few constituents and audience members with the simple treatment and focus**

What you'll soon learn through market research is that the model needs to be much more complex. It needs to acknowledge that changing perception and behavior require a plan that engages more of the audiences who directly interact with the student you are hoping to influence. Your more informed model may look something like Figure 4.2.

In PRISM, our researchers explained in their final report that influencing student achievement depends on supporting and encouraging student interest as part of a cycle of reinforcement (Figure 4.3):

> We believe there is a cycle of reinforcement through which an interest in math and/or science can be enhanced by means of positive experiences and success in those subjects. Similarly, achievement in those subjects can be enhanced by building interest in those subjects. This concept of a virtuous circle of reinforcement informs our ideas for communications strategies and areas of engagement with various audiences. (Maguire 2005)

From our research in Georgia, parents can reinforce the importance of science and mathematics by "providing or identifying appropriate levels and types of support for their children, engaging more with their children in planning their education and exploring career opportunities, and engaging with people in the education community to help champion educational approaches than better match the interests and learning styles of their children" (Maguire 2005).

Another important finding in Georgia was an interesting dichotomy of parents and student perception on "who" had the greatest influence on student choices and behavior. As suspected, parents believed that their child's teachers and school-level administrators had more influence than they themselves (Figure 4.4).

Surprisingly, however, students assessed their parents as having greater influence in their lives over teachers, friends, and other family members (Figure 4.5).

At the conclusion of the eight months, the market research, the thrust of our Public Awareness Campaign in Georgia, then focused on the parents—as chief influencers of their children to help increase students' interest in science and mathematics. From research, strategies were learned for engaging parents, students, educators, business leaders, the community at-large, and anyone else interested in student achievement in science and mathematics. It was learned that what turned out to be a public communications campaign was much more than an *awareness* campaign (Maguire 2005).

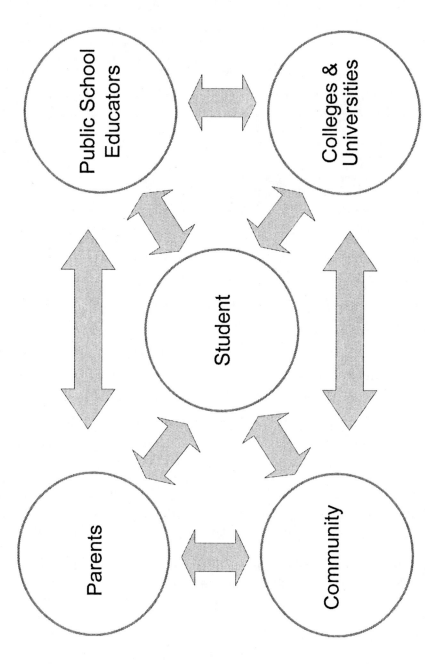

**Figure 4.2.  Modified model of treating a few constituents and audience members**

# A Cycle of Reinforcement

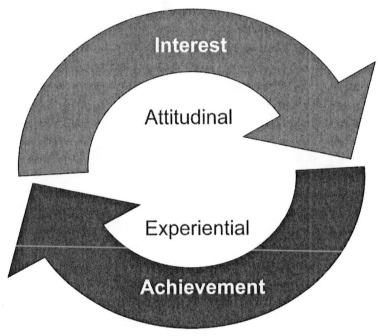

Figure 4.3.    Cycle of reinforcement

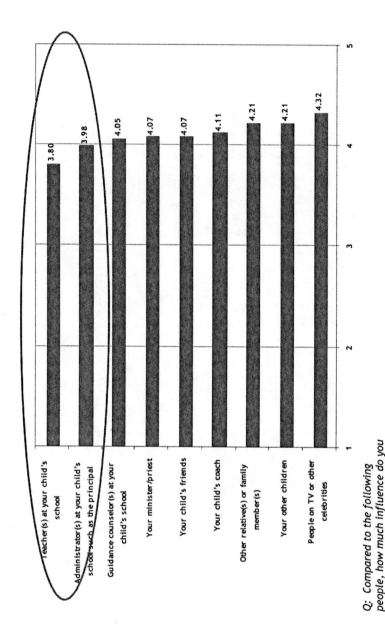

Q: Compared to the following people, how much influence do you think you (and your partner/spouse if applicable) have on your child's formal education?

Scale: 1 = I have much much less influence to 5 = I have much much more influence

**Figure 4.4. Parents' perceptions of influencers on student choices and behavior**

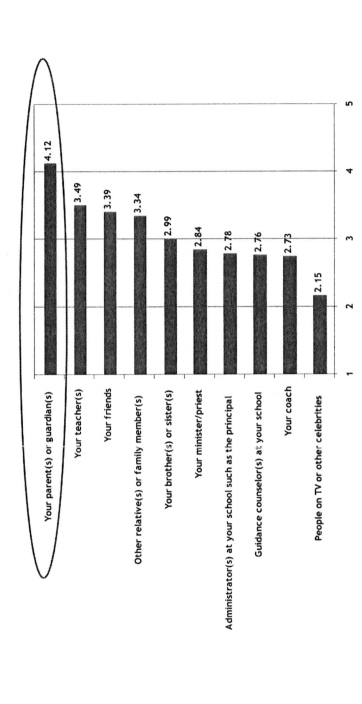

Q: *Please rate how influential each of the following people is on your interest and achievement in school.*

Scale: 1 = Not at all influential to 5 = Extremely influential

**Figure 4.5.   Students' perceptions of influencers on student choices and behavior**

## HOW TO BUILD A COMMUNICATIONS PROGRAM TO INCREASE STUDENT INTEREST IN SCIENCE AND MATHEMATICS

A major recommendation is that you find campaign partners to help you build a communications program that incorporates the findings of market research and that (a) conveys the many messages suggested by the market researchers; (b) exhibits an appealing yet bold expression to attract a broad target audience; and (c) appears to be a big budget campaign but actually uses limited funding.

### Making "Market Research" a "Marketing Reality"

Finding the right public relations firm, advertising agency, and media buyer organization make all of the difference in helping you interpret the market research in such a way that the campaign soars the instant it is launched publicly. You need a full team of vendors to establish your communications plan. Once assembled this team can help you:

- Create and test print advertising and marketing collateral;
- Share market research findings through Public Relations;
- Begin "soft launch" of the Public Awareness Campaign by introducing the concept and desired outcomes to the media;
- Create and test broadcast advertising and marketing collateral;
- Begin "full public launch" of the Public Awareness Campaign on morning news programs;
- Place print advertising material across your state;
- Begin broadcasting TV and radio spots;
- Disseminate resource materials to schools, community organizations;
- Participate in regional activities to promote science and mathematics concepts to community and civic organizations and businesses;
- Conduct market research retest to assess campaign effectiveness and message recall;
- Modify print, broadcast, and resource materials based upon market research findings;
- Continue campaign community outreach and marketing efforts;
- Find ways to directly reach target audiences;
- Share resource materials with others;
- Source corporate funding to begin sustainability efforts;
- Conduct final market research findings; and

- Replicate your Public Awareness Campaign throughout all regions of your state while you continue to seek private funding for ongoing efforts.

In the beginning you find mixed support for conducting a Public Awareness Campaign. Since most schools, colleges, and state education agencies rarely use public engagement activities to encourage change in behavior and perceptions, it is important for your campaign director to spend time and effort trying to convince many members of your state's STEM leadership team that the Public Awareness Campaign can help them achieve their goals.

Spending time interpreting the market research and making sure you are accurately using the researchers' recommendations to develop concepts, collateral, press releases, and placement ideas helps to erase any remembrance of how long it took to get everything started. The advertising agency that assisted the work in Georgia encapsulated their task into one memorable mantra—"develop a campaign that would see more Georgia students taking more math and science courses—especially those with more rigor" (MindPower 2005).

The day the advertisers unveiled the new logo, it seemed like a dream come true. The logo was simple yet elegant. Made to look like a patch, PRISM's new formula for *success* was embodied in the new Public Awareness Campaign logo and accompanying collateral. The University System of Georgia has since trademarked this logo (Figure 4.6). Creating such a logo in your state is an important component of a successful campaign.

It is also important to spend the time necessary to recruit local talent so that all of your print and broadcast materials feature real students from your

**Figure 4.6.  PRISM logo**

state. Staging the launch of your campaign is likewise important. Showcase the concepts you are developing to all of your state education partners. Each time you unveil a new concept to your partners, new information and suggestions are likely to surface. So that by the time you actually launch your campaign you are assured of wide-spread support.

## Retooling for Success

Once your campaign is launched, it may seem like all you need to do is to sustain it. Wrong! Several months after the public launch of your Public Awareness Campaign, it is important for your market researchers to conduct online surveys of parents in the regions of your state where the advertising occurred to see if there is "message recall." Such post-launch data help you to refine your collateral messages and consider new ways to get the messages to your intended audiences.

In the experience through PRISM, some 500 plus parents in Georgia responded to postcards sent to a cross section of families across the state that lived in the neighborhoods exposed to the marketing efforts. The online survey sought to gather information about individual outdoor ads, public service announcements, as well as the print material given to parents and students.

The post-launch research showed (a) the bulk of materials for parents were stored on a Web site that few parents used; (b) in the one region where the community fully embraced the campaign's effort, there was greater success with the materials; (c) the ads resonated more with minorities and those without a college education, two of the key targets of the campaign; (d) the public service announcements were more appealing and matched with parents' preference on how to receive this kind of information; and (e) one form of the outdoor ads yielded the strongest message recall and understanding (Maguire 2007).

The market researchers gave us several recommendations on how to address these findings that helped us make some redirection that proved to be very important. One recommendation was to develop a stronger call to action within all of the materials. There was a general sense that if parents and other interested adults could be convinced in recognizing that the main thrust was to provide information rather than trying to "sell" anything, then there would be an increase in the number of visits to and downloads from the campaign's Web site. The two examples below make the point (Figures 4.7 and 4.8).

**Figure 4.7.   Advertorial at initial public launch**

With this slight change, "Free Parent Guide," there was increased traffic to the campaign Web site as well as an increase in the number of material requests and collateral downloads available to the general public. Another suggestion from the researchers was to vigorously pursue placing a parent guide in the hands of every parent of a child at a PRISM partner school (Figure 4.9). In addition to providing copies of our guides through the Web site, the researchers suggested that developing more grade-level-targeted materials to assist parents with supporting their child's academic efforts also be examined.

To address these recommendations, two different strategies were pursued. With targeted grade-level materials, separate parent guides for elementary school, middle school, and high school students were developed.

**Figure 4.8.   Advertorial after market research findings and recommendations**

**Figure 4.9. Original Parent "Pocket Guide" available when the Public Awareness Campaign was launched**

All guides are used to inform parents about supporting their child's math and science education (Figure 4.10).

If you develop such guides for parents and want to be sure you are placing as many as possible in the hands of parents who want them (and even those who have not thought about it), a recommendation is that you launch an old idea called Math and Science Family Nights.

Although touted as a family night event, it is important to encourage schools to host evening, weekend, or daytime events that invite parents to the school to participate in math and science activities *with* their children. Perhaps you could introduce a mini-grant program and make it available to all elementary, middle, and high schools in your school district, or it could be done statewide.

If you do use a mini-grant approach to provide an incentive for teachers and principals to host Math and Science Family Nights, it is important to invite the applications from the teachers. To build additional buy-in, you could stipulate in your call for mini-grant proposals that you want a team of

**Figure 4.10.** New parent guides developed as a result of the market research

two teachers to serve as Math and Science Family Night coordinators and that they need the support of their principal.

Each mini-grant applicant should be required to submit a description of the planned event, a detailed event timeline as well as a budget outlining how the funds would be used. In addition, you could stipulate that the Math and Science Family Night has to feature math or science learning activities that the student and the parent or guardian must complete together.

Finally, you could stipulate that all mini-grant recipients must (a) disseminate your Public Awareness Campaign materials to parent and guardian attendees; (b) connect all activities to your state or local school system's curriculum standards in science and mathematics; (c) collect evaluations from parent and guardian participants; and (d) provide any additional items that complete a report of activities to the Public Awareness Campaign office.

During the first year of the Math and Science Family Night mini-grant program, fifty events were held throughout the PRISM schools with an attendance of 8,405, with 1,600 parent evaluations collected (Figure 4.11 and 4.12).

The important point of including Math and Science Family Nights in your campaign is to influence parents' understanding of the importance of their support of their child's science and mathematics education. If your experience mirrors ours, you find that many schools provide materials to families to encourage parents to conduct science experiments and math challenges at home with their children. You also find that parents are able to connect with their child's teacher and school administrator in a non-threatening manner, thereby improving parent-teacher interactions. Finally, you find that Math and Science Family Nights help to drive home one of the most important messages of your campaign and market research findings—that science and mathematics are part of everyday life and that these subjects can be fun.

The Math and Science Family Night mini-grant program was found to be a resounding success in Georgia as many schools used these events as opportunities to engage parents in non-threatening environments. During the second year of the mini-grant program, schools that were first-year recipients, agreed to receive only half of the funding ($250) the second year, agreeing to seek a match of $250 from corporate partners and businesses in their communities.

### Example: Sampling of Parent Comments in Georgia

- Have Math and Science Family Night early in the school year so the children can apply the knowledge they are learning throughout the entire

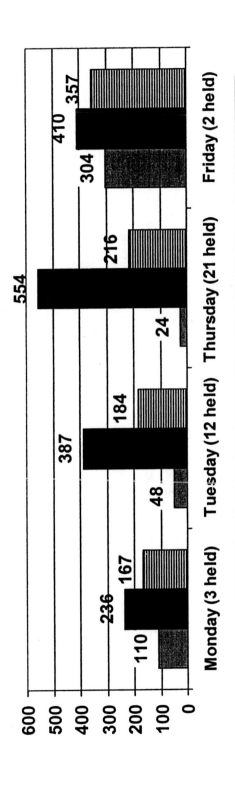

Figure 4.11. 2006–2007 attendance for elementary school Math and Science Family Nights

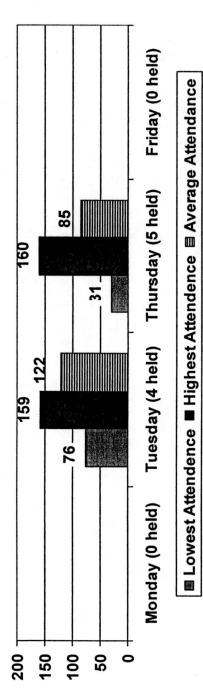

**Figure 4.12.** 2006–2007 attendance for middle school Math and Science Family Nights

year, and the parents can work with their children at home throughout
the entire year

- Have a separate night for math and a separate night for science so
  there is an applicable amount of time to do the activities and experiments (or both math and science on a Friday or the weekend)
- Hold the Family Night between 6:00 pm and 8:00 pm so parents have
  enough time to get off work, and it ends in time for smaller children to
  make their bed times
- Do not have a PTA meeting beforehand, this makes the children rest-
  less and it takes up time that could be spent doing activities and experiments
- Provide child care for little brothers and sisters so they are not making
  noise and crowding the activity and experiment areas
- Make sure to advertise in plenty of places (school newspapers, posters,
  e-mails to parents) so the parents are aware of the night in plenty of
  time to make arrangements
- Send reminders to parents a week beforehand
- Have the advertisements, reminders, activities and experiments, and
  evaluations in Spanish (if applicable)
- Have prizes for completing the activities and experiments for the children. This gives the children incentive to come to the night and have
  fun learning (a free homework pass or receiving a ticket after a completed experiment to enter a door prize)
- Have a book or handout to take home that has a summary of all the activities and experiments as well as the facts about the standardized
  tests

### Using a High School Teaching Initiative to Increase Student Interest in Science and Mathematics

At the high school level, a recommended strategy is to stimulate student
interest in teaching science and mathematics through creating an Advanced
Academy for Future Teachers (AAFT). Through PRISM, the Atlanta Public Schools and Georgia State University created an AAFT to recruit bright,
talented, and diverse rising junior and senior high school students to consider science and mathematics teaching as a rewarding career. A secondary
goal of the program was to help high school students to develop insights
about teachers and schools so that they could understand the nature of elementary and secondary science and mathematics.

If you decide to start an AAFT, it is important in your design to include opportunities for high school students to collaborate with university faculty and master teachers, to develop teaching and tutoring skills, to participate in educational seminars and workshops, and to experience opportunities for academic and professional preparation. High school student participants should be required to do presentations so they are able to develop insights into teaching and to learn leadership skills. AAFT students should have opportunities for academic and professional exploration and growth, and for reflection and self-discovery.

### Recruitment into AAFT

Students should be recruited jointly by a school district and nearby university. Eligibility criteria should include: a minimum GPA of 2.5, an original essay by the student, and recommendations from two of their high school teachers. A K-16 selection committee is recommended to select qualifying participants and to send them invitations to attend AAFT. In our experience in Atlanta, the composition of our participants was as follows:

**Table 4.1.  Participants in AAFT by gender and ethnicity for 2007 (based on survey data)**

| Gender or Ethnicity | 2007 (N=42) |
| --- | --- |
| Male | 14% |
| Female | 85% |
| African American | 98% |
| Asian | 1% |

### Findings from the AAFT in Atlanta

There are three years of data on the AAFT in Atlanta. The AAFT survey was administered each year during one of the final two days of the AAFT program so response rates have been nearly 100 percent. Here are the findings:

- On the average, over 69 percent of all AAFT participants reported that AAFT either had reinforced their decision to become a teacher or made them want to become a teacher, with 57 percent interested in science or mathematics teaching.
- Another 16 percent indicated an interest in a science- or math-related field, but not in teaching.

- Survey results, interviews, and observations demonstrate that students overwhelmingly enjoyed the science and mathematics activities in AAFT.
- Of those interested in teaching, 51 percent of AAFT students said they were interested in a career in teaching early childhood and elementary grades; 14 percent self-reported an interest in middle school teaching; and 33 percent indicated an interest in teaching high school (Ngari et al. 2008).
- Twenty percent of the 2006 participants and 32 percent of the 2007 participants indicated that they learned specific new mathematics content.
- Twenty-seven percent of the 2006 participants and 56 percent of the 2007 participants indicated that they learned specific new science content.
- To date, 109 AAFT participants (34, 49, and 26 for 2004, 2005, and 2006, respectively) have graduated from high school.
- Of the 109 high school graduates, college enrollment for 60 students (55 percent) was in USG institutions and the remainder might have attended college out of state since all reported they planned to attend college.
- Of those in USG institutions, 75 percent of AAFT graduates enrolled in four-year degree-awarding colleges and 25 percent in non-degree colleges (this statistic matched what the students had indicated in the AAFT survey about their desire to attend college).
- Eleven out of sixteen (69 percent) contacted by telephone indicated they are interested in teaching, again supporting their earlier indications on the AAFT survey. Some of the education and teaching fields revealed were early childhood education, biology, music, and secondary education.

## SUSTAINING EFFORTS THAT PROMOTE STUDENT INTEREST, CHOICES, AND ACHIEVEMENT IN SCIENCE AND MATHEMATICS

Unlike the famed "Got Milk?" awareness effort that enjoyed seed funding from the California Milk Processor Board and eventual support from dairy boards across North America, most awareness campaigns are burdened with the prospect of never being able to find a sustainable force to keep them afloat for decades (Holt 2002).

Needless to say, the development of a broad-based public awareness campaign—that includes communications materials and events—requires resources coupled with committed partners who are willing to define and refine target audience messages and programs to make sure the campaign goals are reached. Such initiatives must also show evidence of measurable affect on the attitudes and perceptions you hope to change—in this case increased student interest in science and mathematics.

Since increasing student interest in science and mathematics is not a one-shot thing, it is important from the outset to focus concurrently on launching your campaign and related programs and on seeking sustainable funding. If your experience mirrors ours, you find that once you get materials and programs in place, many states and educational agencies ask if they can use the materials you've developed or borrow the associated concepts. In this situation, it is important to walk a fine line between altruism—for the common good—and having the needed resources to sustain your own work. Some sort of cost-share arrangement makes the most sense to us, where other states pay a fee to be able to reproduce your materials, with the income from the fee going to sustain the work at home.

Another suggestion you could try to generate additional funding for this work is to develop a DVD series on planning and implementing school-based Math and Science Family Nights or on designing and running an Advanced Academy for Future Teachers. These how-to DVDs could serve not only as a revenue source for you to sustain your work, but also to get some of your critical findings into public schools across the nation. This, in turn, can help to proliferate the message of getting families involved, and to include students, themselves, in programs designed to increase their interest and achievement in science and mathematics.

Another suggestion on how to secure funding to sustain your work is to seek corporate partners who may wish to participate in your campaign through using various co-branded collateral items to suggest their support of STEM education and statewide efforts to encourage student interest in these fields. While this has the greatest possible potential regarding continuing the advertorial aspects of the campaign, it is the most difficult to pursue. As new corporations have been considered for approach, those corporations that want to make sure their dollars work for sustainable efforts and programs that influence student and parent choice, and not just one-time ads that may not reach the audience intended, are the most likely to be receptive. Having solid data from your market researchers about increased student interest in science and mathematics resulting from your campaign materials, Math and Science Family Nights, and such programs as the Advance Academy for Future Teachers, helps minimize these fears and maximize your success to sustain this work.

## SUMMARY OF HOW TO DEVELOP AN AWARENESS CAMPAIGN AND ADVANCED ACADEMY FOR FUTURE TEACHERS PROGRAM

### Public Awareness Campaign:

- Conduct Market Research in your area to plan for relevant nuances in your community.
- Assemble a campaign team that assists with developing a comprehensive communications plan that includes message development, public relations, advertising and marketing, media placement, and a research and evaluation component.
- Be sure to test and retest your collateral materials with state and educational partners as well as the intended audiences. Be ready and willing to make suggested changes—especially those suggestions that come from your target audience (they actually know what works for them).
- Carefully plan where, when, and how you showcase your advertising material.
- Develop material that can be used in a number of ways by several different audiences.
- Be sure to place your material on a Web site and encourage visitors to download what you've created—this spurs interest and expands your campaign beyond your reach.
- Include elements within your campaign that help you get the message out to your target audience (such as Family Nights or other activities).
- Find ways to connect with organizations and corporations interested in helping you advance your efforts and the campaign.
- Whenever possible, seek to connect your campaign to a larger initiative to make sure all of the basics associated with excelling in mathematics and science are being addressed (such as teacher professional development, teacher rewards, etc.).

### Advanced Academy for Future Teachers (AAFT):

- When starting an AAFT program, it is best to find a school that has a background in providing students career training and exploration experiences that also include summer enrichment opportunities—this helps expedite the eventual "launch" of your program.

- Be sure to partner with a college or university interested in a long-term commitment of developing a potential pipeline of students desiring teaching as a career.
- Recruit students early and often—look for students who excel in science or mathematics as well as those who express interest in teaching and tutoring.
- Whenever possible, make sure the program can operate during the school year so that the summer sessions are relevant and worthwhile.
- AAFT works best with older high school students (rising and current eleventh and twelfth graders).
- Address travel and summer work plans by offering stipends and travel vouchers for students. Typically eleventh- and twelfth-grade students have some kind of summer job to help supplement their buying needs during the school year—providing stipends helps allay concerns about not being able to earn money over the summer.
- Find school year and summer instructors who have a passion for learning and teaching—instructors who enjoy working with students eager to try untested styles and methods of instruction.
- Include field trips and other outside-of-the-classroom experiences that enrich the program activities.
- Hold ceremonial events at the end of the year to reward (and encourage) students for their hard work for the year prior.

## NOTE

1. Rosalind Barnes Fowler is the public awareness director in the Partnership for Reform In Science and Mathematics (PRISM), a systemic K–16 STEM initiative in Georgia. She is a project director and communications professional in the P–16 department for the University System of Georgia.

# 5

# BUILDING CAPACITY FOR IMPROVING TEACHING QUALITY

*Dava C. Coleman*[1]

## INTRODUCTION

There is little dispute in education that teacher effectiveness is a major contributing factor to improving student learning (Darling-Hammond and Post 2000). So improving teacher effectiveness is a primary mechanism for increasing student learning in science and mathematics. This chapter proposes a professional development blueprint for improving teaching and learning in STEM fields based on lessons learned from the research literature and through practice in Georgia's Partnership for Reform In Science and Mathematics (PRISM). The proposed blueprint includes the following elements:

- Collaborative partnerships
- Explicit student learning standards
- Improved classroom practices

The formation of collaborative partnerships, particularly those involving members from both K–12 and higher education, is discussed in chapter 2. Strategies for development of explicit learning standards are described in chapter 3. This chapter focuses on the third element, improved classroom practices, and how professional development activities are designed to increase teaching effectiveness.

## PRINCIPLES OF TEACHER PROFESSIONAL DEVELOPMENT

Figure 5.1 illustrates the principles of professional development that can lead to improved classroom practices and ultimately to improved student learning.

It is well-documented that not all teacher professional learning directly improves student achievement (Joyce and Showers 2002). So, increasing the achievement level of mathematics and science students requires significant reform in what teachers know and in how they teach. In turn, this requires significant reform in how teachers themselves are taught. Let's examine each of the three principles in Figure 5.1 in detail.

### Integrating Content and Pedagogy: Balance is Everything!

Improving student learning requires teachers who have adequate content knowledge and pedagogical content knowledge. It has been shown that teachers cannot teach students content beyond their own understanding (Ma 1999). According to Cohen and Hill (1998), professional development activities that focus on content acquisition alone may improve mathematical or scientific understanding, but do not necessarily result in higher levels of student learning. Cohen and Hill submit that the content teachers need to learn is the content they have to teach. If there is a balance between the content and pedagogy in the professional development activity, teachers connect the content they are learning with how they should teach it to their students. Thus, an integrated focus for professional development activities

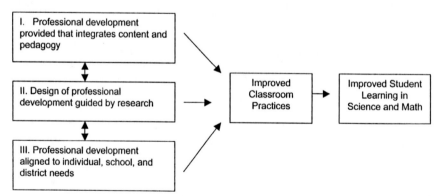

**Figure 5.1.  Principles of professional development that can lead to improved classroom practices and student learning success**

is a good way to enhance both as opposed to separate professional development activities for each.

For example, the state of Georgia set out to improve mathematics teaching and learning in elementary schools by designing an endorsement program to be taught to all pre-service elementary teachers. The question then was posed: Why not offer this endorsement in mathematics to current elementary teachers? The plan was to implement a mathematics endorsement for in-service elementary teachers that would include four courses: Numbers and Operations, Data Analysis and Probability, Algebra, and Geometry. The content-focused courses were designed by a consortium of mathematics and mathematics education faculty from several University System of Georgia institutions. The instructors of these courses were to be university mathematics faculty.

However, the result was that while the endorsement courses were easily implemented to pre-service elementary teachers, it was not as easy to make them available for in-service teachers. The challenge existed for several reasons. First, offering them as university courses meant that in-service teachers would have to be admitted to the university and the courses would have to be scheduled for the late afternoon or evening. Second, many of the in-service elementary teachers were reluctant to take a "content course" because of perceived difficulty level. Third, teachers believed that a content course would not be relevant to what they needed to teach (Gilbert et al. 2008).

In discussing the extremely low enrollment in these mathematics courses for in-service courses, it was recognized that the in-service teachers might enroll in the endorsement program if: (1) a balance between content and pedagogy was evident; (2) courses were offered on a teacher-friendly schedule; and (3) the courses were taught by a team of mathematics professors and K–12 mathematics educators with advanced degrees. Working with a local Regional Education Service Agency (RESA), all four courses were modified to engage teachers in the mathematics as students and to include discussions of pedagogy around the mathematical concepts. A field experience component was also added to connect the coursework with the teachers' classrooms. Evaluation results showed an increase in content knowledge as measured by pre- and post-test assessments and a change in mathematics teaching practice (Gilbert et al. 2008).

***Example: Modifications of the Georgia Mathematics Endorsement for In-Service Elementary Teachers.*** The Georgia Mathematics Endorsement for elementary teachers is comprised of four courses—Numbers and Operations, Algebra, Geometry, and Data Analysis and Probability. In addition to the mathematics content goals in each course, as the Endorsement Program was redesigned for in-service elementary teachers, the latter were expected to meet the following pedagogical goals:

- Solve problems using multiple strategies; interpret solutions; determine reasonableness of answer.
- Nurture collaboration, critical thinking, hands-on exploration, implementation addressing various learning styles.
- Select and use a variety of formative and summative assessments to monitor student progress.

In addition to classwork, a field experience provided an opportunity for teachers to design and implement lessons highlighting the above goals.

As you design professional development, make the content of the activity contextual for teachers by blending content with pedagogy. Provide opportunities for the teachers to try out new strategies and discuss the impact on student learning. Finally, provide building-level and school-district-level support for teachers to engage in professional development and to implement new teaching practices.

## Designing Research-Based Professional Development—One Size Never Fits All!

Planning professional development for teachers strikes fear in the heart of most educators. They continually ask themselves, "Is this what is needed?" "Will the teachers respond well to what I have planned?" "Is this a repeat of what teachers have already heard?" "Will teachers take away the same outcomes as those I intend?" "Will they have enough experience during the professional development to enable them to implement successfully in their classrooms?" "Will there be continuing support for the work after the workshop is over?"

All of these questions and many more haunt professional developers as they struggle to plan effective teacher professional learning. The simple truth is that there is no one model for designing and implementing professional learning that will guarantee results in improved student learning. This is true because designing and implementing effective professional development is setting-dependent (Loucks-Horsley et al. 2003). You must consider the unique goals, strengths, resources, and barriers within the setting for which you are planning.

First, to implement a systematic professional development program, you need to create or adopt a framework to guide the design process. Who provides input? How will decisions be made? What professional development will be offered? How will it be evaluated? These are just a few of the questions that should be addressed. Providing opportunities for teachers to provide input is essential.

A framework that is particularly useful is one proposed in *Designing Professional Development for Teachers of Science and Mathematics* (Loucks-Horsley et al. 2003). The framework outlines a design plan that includes:

- Committing to a vision and standards;
- Analyzing student learning and other data;
- Setting goals by identifying critical issues;
- Planning the strategies to be used to accomplish the goals;
- Doing the professional development activity; and
- Evaluating its impact.

***Committing to a Vision and Standards.***   As soon as the leadership team is in place for your STEM initiative (as defined in chapter 2), your team should commit to a vision and standards for teacher professional learning. Prior to doing this, it is highly recommended that your team spend time together reviewing the professional development research together. For example, you could examine the National Staff Development Council's (2001) *Standards for Staff Development* and *Designing Powerful Professional Development for Teachers and Principals* (Sparks 2002). You could also examine current cognitive research on how to support transformative learning for teachers, such as *How People Learn: Brain, Mind, Experience, and School* (Bransford et al. 1999). When your team collaboratively completes such a literature review, all members gain a clearer focus and purpose for professional learning across your region. See the example below for the statement of guiding principles developed by three school districts and two higher education institutions in one of the PRISM regions in Georgia.

***Example: Guiding Principles for Mathematics and Science Professional Learning.***   The PRISM Northeast Georgia Regional Coordinating Committee believes that professional learning for teachers is the primary avenue for increasing student learning in mathematics and science. For professional learning to impact teacher classroom practice and to enhance teacher quality in content and pedagogy, the following principles for teacher professional learning must be present.

Professional learning activities for teachers must provide opportunities for teachers to:

1. Reflect on their practices and student learning individually and with colleagues.
2. Experience learning actively in the manner in which people learn best.
3. Engage in real work that is contextual and related directly to teaching.
4. Learn collaboratively with kindergarten through college colleagues.
5. Evaluate their performance as well as the performance of their students.

Specifically, professional learning must be evidence-based, relate to the implementation of the Georgia Performance Standards, and be structured for a period of time that allows for a process of teacher learning, classroom implementation, reflection, and collaborative discussion.

Your leadership team could also set a common vision for teacher professional learning through criteria for evaluating professional development proposals and then award funds accordingly. Your leadership team could establish explicit criteria and appoint a review committee, composed of Lead Teachers, higher education faculty, and your regional leadership team.

***Example: Characteristics of Professional Development in Another PRISM Region.***    PRISM Professional Development is to be data-driven, content-based, collaborative with higher education, and driven completely by teacher needs as communicated through the regional network of learning communities. This statement mirrors the definition of PRISM professional development as written by the statewide leadership team.

The following review criteria were intended to help ensure that all regional PRISM supported professional development involve these defining aspects:

1. The proposed professional development opportunity deepens the science or mathematics content knowledge of participating teachers. It is directly connected to K–12 science and mathematics standards. Professional development participants exhibit ability to apply teaching styles appropriate to a variety of audiences relative to this content.
2. The proposed professional development opportunity is based upon data and evidence of need. Test scores and other data are used to identify very specific strands of student weakness. Multiple indicators are used as evidence of need.

3. The proposed opportunity involves higher education faculty. Such faculty should be involved in at least one of the following: determining need, planning the activities, delivery, or follow-up. K–12 and higher education faculty work collaboratively on every aspect of the professional development opportunity: determining need, planning the activities, delivery, and follow-up.

4. The proposed opportunity is developed within a PRISM learning community. Professional development is planned by and occurs within a PRISM learning community. Ongoing reflection and discussion of classroom impact occur within a PRISM learning community. Impact of the professional development is shared within and outside of the region through meeting presentations and journal articles.

5. The proposal is tied to relevant literature. The proposed professional development opportunity is research-based with documented evidence of effectiveness within similar classroom settings. Several citations are given.

6. The proposed opportunity leads to changes in instructional practice, classroom climate, and student learning. Positive change in student achievement is measured and documented. Multiple indicators are used to measure classroom impact.

Each of these examples illustrates how a clear vision and standards for professional learning ensure the design and implementation of effective professional development.

*Analyzing Student Learning and Other Data.* In this era of school accountability, the focus of schools and their communities is on student achievement scores. But, reforming teaching to improve student learning does not happen by magic. It takes an inquiry-based approach that begins and ends with data. So, the second step in the design process is to anchor your professional development work with an inquiry into data from multiple sources. Data useful to the enhancement of professional development include standardized test scores, performance assessment results, student work, teacher surveys, and classroom observations, among others. In her guidebook, *Using Data/Getting Results: A Practical Guide for School Improvement in Mathematics and Science,* Love (2002) outlines a process for using data systematically to examine teaching practices and student learning.

She identifies six phases in a cycle of collaborative inquiry: framing the question, collecting data, analyzing data, organizing data-driven dialogue, drawing conclusions and taking action, and monitoring results. One data analysis technique in which to engage your teachers and administrators at the school or district level is "data-driven dialogue" (Wellman and Lipton 2004).

If you decide to follow the *Using Data* process developed by Love (2002), you should find that it provides a process to improve student achievement in mathematics and science based on working with teachers to use multiple levels and types of data. Through professional development, data teams can be formed to learn about the process and to engage in data-based collaborative inquiry. At the school level, each participating school could add a Data Facilitator to existing teams charged with strategy development for improving student learning and achievement in science and mathematics. The data facilitators could conduct quarterly data dialogues with teachers at the school. Data Facilitator Workshops could be designed to prepare facilitators to redeliver the strategies during summer professional development.

### Example: What Teachers Say about Using "Data-Driven Dialogue"

I used to think . . . *data was used by the county to compare schools to schools.*
But now I think . . . *data is a tool to drive instruction.*
I used to think . . . *teachers could not find time to analyze data.*
But now I think . . . *there is definitely enough time to sit down to look over the data. It is a vital process that must be done.*
I used to think . . . *data was used to determine pass or fail.*
But now I think . . . *it is helpful to identify areas of strengths and weaknesses and where I can best help my students.*

**Setting Goals by Identifying Critical Issues.** "The process of data analysis should lead the professional development team to a small number of specific, attainable, and measurable student learning goals" (Loucks-Horsley et al. 2003, 23). Look for standards or learning outcomes in subjects where achievement is low because goals should target the standards or learning outcomes (Schmoker 2002). Ideally, professional development goals should be for student learning, teacher learning, teaching practice, or the organization, such as implementing learning communities or training Lead Teachers. Having specific measurable goals sets the stage for evaluation in the last step of the framework (Loucks-Horsley et al. 2003, 23).

**Planning, Doing, and Evaluating the Professional Development.** Planning, doing, and evaluating are the three final steps in the framework. There are several important issues to keep in mind as you plan and implement professional development.

Consider teachers' background knowledge and contextual issues specific to the school or district. Meeting the needs of teachers in a time that is convenient and consistent with how adults learn is critical. Earlier in this chapter, the redesign of the Mathematics Endorsement program for in-service elementary teachers was discussed as an example of balancing content knowledge with pedagogy. It is also an excellent illustration of the importance of considering contextual issues. The original design identified four university-based courses to be taught by mathematics professors. Being taught as a mathematics course did not appeal to teachers nor was it convenient to enroll in a university to take the courses. The redesign made the courses more job-embedded and they were offered on a teacher friendly schedule.

Involve your higher education faculty partners in the planning stages. Their input is critical and they develop a vested interest in the success of the professional development activity. Too often higher education faculty are brought in to "do" the professional development activity without a real understanding of the goals to be accomplished or why they are the goals. Taking the time and effort to involve higher education faculty initially should produce a better experience for the teachers.

For example, one PRISM school district wanted to design a professional learning workshop for grades 9–12 science teachers and grade 6 mathematics teachers who were implementing a new standards-based statewide curriculum. The goals of the workshop were to explore the new Georgia Performance Standards, develop curriculum for those standards, and develop performance-based assessments. The district coordinator organized a planning group that included lead teacher facilitators, science and mathematics district coordinators, and higher education faculty from STEM and the College of Education. However, the district coordinator felt that an educational consultant whom she had met at a conference would be valuable and enlisted her services without the planning group's input.

During the initial planning meeting, the district coordinator deferred to the consultant, which resulted in a tension for the higher education faculty who thought they were brought in for their expertise. Ultimately, the workshop design produced was very successful. Each morning began with a general presentation related to standards-based teaching and assessment conducted by the consultant. This was followed by discipline-specific group time. Each group was led by a three-person team consisting of a STEM higher education faculty member, a higher education science or mathematics educator, and a lead teacher. These teams became responsible for accomplishing the goals of the workshop.

At the end of each day of the workshop, all teams met together to discuss progress and review plans for the next day's activities. Although the workshop was successful, the lesson learned for this district was to organize the planning team early and make key decisions collaboratively. Another interesting note to add is the impact on the university faculty. One university faculty member said that she had a better understanding of what teachers needed:

> I have a new sense for the kinds of ongoing outreach activities that teachers are interested in, and have been planning workshops, seminars, and even developing assessments for training other graduate students and faculty.

She also said that this experience had significantly affected her practice, particularly in her assessment methods.

> The interactions begun and fostered in this program have led to a complete change in how I teach my courses. As a result of the program, I received NSF funding to completely redesign the intro Bio curriculum to utilize an inquiry approach. Most importantly, though, I gained some incredible knowledge about how to assess the labs. Without this support, I doubt I could have accomplished such a major paradigm shift in how we are teaching our courses, nor could I have critically investigated if they were causing real improvement in student learning.

Lesson study is also a very useful way to organize teacher professional learning. Although it is a relatively new approach in the United States, it provides a structure for teachers to collaboratively plan, implement, observe, and revise a lesson according to the model described by Lewis (2002). A major focus of this type of professional development is the content-based dialogue in which teachers engage.

When forming lesson study groups it is recommended that teachers form grade-level–lesson-study teams and that they meet during common planning time. In PRISM, the groups met seven times during the first cycle of lesson study, teaching and re-teaching the lesson before winter break. They met four times during the second cycle of lesson study, teaching and re-teaching the lesson before spring break.

These teachers were all new to lesson study, having only been introduced to the process during pre-planning, and they had not previously belonged to a professional learning community. The groups were facilitated by a person outside the district, who is a mathematics educator and experienced lesson study facilitator. Also, a professor of mathematics education, with expertise in lesson study, participated on public teaching days, observing the lesson and advising the groups during the revision process for the public teaching of the revised lesson.

Participating in the lesson study in collaborative groups for a total of twenty to twenty-five weeks during the school year allowed the teachers to learn from each other. The meetings focused the teachers on a particular lesson, the mathematical content of the lesson, the state standards addressed by the lesson, and the evidence the teachers should be able to gather with regard to what the students were learning during the lesson. The teachers used this collaborative time working inside the lesson, ironing out the structure and details of it, articulating reasons for their choices in the work. Discussing professional work for that length of time in such detail provided the negotiation of knowledge that is intrinsic to professional learning communities.

In this lesson study example, the teachers did not follow the tradition of a two-day how-to workshop where participants are left to make what they can of research and agendas. Instead, these teachers were taught about the process of lesson study while they were participating in lesson study, being guided by an experienced facilitator. The structure was put in place and maintained by the facilitator, leaving for them the role of learner. This role included learning about lesson study and learning about the practice of mathematics teaching and learning.

Therefore, the group as a learning community gained knowledge of a professional learning experience and knowledge about teaching and learning mathematics. If you use the lesson study method, you should find that as knowledge of this experience becomes deep and flexible, the stage is set for further exploration into the teaching and learning of mathematics and the expansion of this knowledge.

After working so many hours on the preparation of the lesson, the teachers were surprised by what they learned on the day of the public teaching. One teacher exclaimed, "Now I understand what lesson study is about!" The teachers had observed other classes before, both as pre-service and in-service teachers. They expected these observations to be similar. However, none of their previous experiences included a plan truly created by a group. Additionally, the purpose of those earlier experiences was to observe the teacher.

In lesson study, the purpose of the observation is to observe the students in order to determine what and how they are learning. The teachers spent more than eight hours during the first cycle and more than five during the second cycle planning what they expected to be the perfect lesson. Then they observed the implementation of the lesson and witnessed, with evidence, whether or not the goal was achieved. This was a very new lens for the teachers to use, one that they did not expect to be so revealing. Next, the teachers had to reconstruct parts of the lesson, after exploring this critical evidence, and teach a revised lesson planned for greater success.

Finally, the input of the outside expert in mathematics education and lesson study proved to guide much of the revision and to lay the groundwork for further exploration by the teachers. This outside expert, often referred to as the knowledgeable other, was able to look at the lesson as it was taught with a fresh perspective immersed in experience. The dialogue between the knowledgeable other and the teachers focused on the mathematics of the standards and how students may come to experience that mathematics. The teachers carried this experience with the knowledgeable other into the work of the learning community afterwards, using it to inform their continued work.

Although teachers may collaborate with colleagues within buildings regularly, lesson study offers teachers an opportunity to collaborate in a new, focused, detailed manner that must be learned. The experience of these teachers in PRISM provides an example of professional learning that can occur in a learning community whose work is lesson study.

Chapter 8 provides specific information on designing evaluation for professional learning. An excellent resource to consider is *Evaluating Professional Development* by Guskey (2000).

## Aligning Professional Development to School and District Needs—Don't Spread Too Thin!

Regardless of the size of a school district, it is critical that you begin by identifying a focus for professional development based on the needs of students and teachers. A narrow focus allows resources to be concentrated on a small set of improvements rather than spread over many. Then, design and implement professional development opportunities that model research-based practices tied to student learning standards and classroom instruction. As noted previously in this chapter, a variety of professional development models can be utilized and should include customized professional development (rather than one size fits all).

Setting funding priorities is critical because there is never enough money to do what you would like to do. Gather teacher input and focus the available funds on where the need is greatest. To make funding go further, partner with other educational groups in your state and region who have the same need. Earlier examples in this chapter have pointed out the value-added of having higher education institutions be collaborative partners. They are a tremendous resource in providing content and pedagogical expertise. Also, calling on state and local professional developers to provide the knowledge, strategies, and skills needed to train teachers to implement your state's standards is another source of expertise.

As an example of how a local region can partner with your state department of education, one PRISM region, based on survey data and discussions with teachers, identified the new state high school math standards and curriculum as an area of great interest to a variety of teachers and administrators. The leadership team in this region designed a one night professional development activity, High School Math Night. A Mathematics Education Specialist from the Georgia Department of Education was invited to address the participants. She was directed to address the areas of concern that the teachers had, such as the nature of the mathematical tasks to be used and how their lesson planning would need to change. The Mathematics Education Specialist described her personal experience as a classroom teacher in the making of the new standards. She shared her personal testimony on how the state had reached the point they did and why she supports the new standards and curriculum.

The success of this professional development was dependent on several variables. First, a real need was identified using a variety of data sources. Second, communication between the State Department of Education and a regional K–16 STEM leadership team was thorough. Third, the speaker accurately addressed the teachers' needs. The opportunity for high school mathematics teachers, mathematics professors, undergraduate mathematics education students, and Regional Education Service Agency consultants to hear about the new mathematics standards and work together on sample mathematics tasks was critical. Participants from all mathematical backgrounds left the event with greater understanding and an increased comfort level for the new state standards in mathematics.

## Building Teacher Capacity—Your Teachers Are Your Greatest Asset!

It is important to build teacher capacity by providing professional learning that is targeted toward developing teacher leaders and by creating a variety of teacher leader models designed to support teachers.

Each school in your STEM initiative could be encouraged to identify two Lead Teachers—one in science and one in mathematics. The primary goal of Lead Teacher is to provide school leadership for accomplishing your STEM goals. Specifically, their role is to organize and facilitate school-based science and mathematics learning communities and teacher-managed professional learning. Criteria for selection of lead teachers should be the decision of each partner district in your STEM initiative.

If you decide to use a Lead Teacher model, it is important to provide any needed additional support so that teachers may thrive in this new role. One example of support for developing Lead Teachers and to help them build a sense of community is to design a Lead Teacher Academy that is modeled after the National Academy for K–12 Science and Mathematics Education Leadership (1997). The purpose of the Academy is to help leaders of science and mathematics education reform:

- Succeed in planning and improving instruction in science and mathematics.
- Gain knowledge, skills, and strategies for initiating, implementing, and sustaining reform that helps *all* students learn science and mathematics.
- Build a strong, supportive, and ongoing learning community for teachers of science and mathematics.

In your first Lead Teacher Academy, it is important to provide the developing Lead Teachers with an overview of your STEM initiative and to include activities that are focused on effective leadership practices, such as how to use school data to improve science and mathematics instruction and how to lead professional learning. It is also important to provide regional planning time in the daily schedule of the Academy. Each day should begin and end with a self-assessment to encourage the lead teachers to reflect on the day's work and to provide information to those running the Academy.

If additional teachers are moving into Lead Teacher roles, during a second Lead Teacher Academy it is recommended that you bring the veteran lead teachers (who attended the first Academy) to join the new Lead Teachers at the conclusion of the first day. This practice can provide the opportunity for the newly appointed Lead Teachers to catch up with the training provided during the first Academy.

It is also important during the second Academy to involve your veteran Lead Teachers in some leadership role during the second Academy. For example, veteran Lead Teachers could participate in a panel discussion detailing the successes and challenges of being a lead teacher. These kinds of activities can provide the new Lead Teachers an opportunity to hear about the work of Lead Teachers firsthand and to ask questions.

During Lead Teacher Academies, it is important to introduce or to provide opportunities for teachers to develop a deeper understand of a Professional Learning Design Framework (Loucks-Horsley et al. 2003) and how to use it. As mentioned previously, it is also important to begin and end each day in Lead Teacher Academies with a self-assessment to encourage the Lead Teachers to reflect on the day's work and to provide information to the planners.

## CONCLUSION

Professional development is the key to improving teaching quality, but only if it is planned systematically in relation to the goals of the school or school district. It can change the culture of the school from one where teachers make decisions haphazardly and in isolation of their colleagues to one where the whole school focus is on instructional decisions that improve student learning. In summary, there are four steps on the road to building effective teacher professional development:

1. Create or adopt a framework for guiding the design process:
   a. A framework provides a structure for the work of the professional learning committee and guides their decision-making. The framework described in this chapter is one proposed by Loucks-Horsley et al. (2003). The framework involves:

   - Committing to a vision and standards
   - Analyzing student learning and other data
   - Setting goals by identifying critical issues
   - Planning the strategies to be used to accomplish the goals
   - Doing the professional development activity
   - Evaluating the impact of the activity on teacher practice and student learning

2. Align professional development to your school or district needs:
   a. You must identify a focus for professional development based on needs identified through your data analysis. A narrow focus allows limited resources to be concentrated on a small set of improvements rather than spread too thinly over many.

3. Design professional development activities to accomplish your goals
   using research-based practices that integrate content and pedagogy:
   a. Be sure to consider contextual issues, such as teacher background,
      schedule, and place when designing the activities. Involve commu-
      nity resources and higher education faculty partners early in the
      planning stages. Don't be afraid to try new formats for professional
      learning.
4. Involve your teachers in their own professional development:
   a. Build teacher capacity by providing professional learning that is
      targeted toward developing teacher leaders. With a minimum of
      expenses, you can implement any number of teacher leader mod-
      els. On-site mathematics and science "teaching experts" can work
      with collaborative teacher teams and provide small group profes-
      sional learning, in addition to working one-on-one with teachers in
      their classrooms.

## NOTE

1. Dava C. Coleman is a regional director in the Partnership for Reform in Science and Mathematics (PRISM), a systemic K–16 STEM initiative in Georgia. She
is a high school teacher with Jackson County Schools in Jefferson, Georgia.

# 6

# PROFESSIONAL LEARNING COMMUNITIES

*Sabrina A. Hessinger*[1]

## INTRODUCTION

**P**rofessional learning communities are a growing trend among educational institutions across the nation. In many K–12 school systems, professional learning communities are considered the most effective form of teacher development and enhancement. The recent literature identifies several common characteristics of successful professional learning communities. These include shared leadership, shared values and vision, collective learning and application, supportive conditions, and shared practice.

This chapter describes several models for school-college (K–16) professional learning communities, ranging from school-based to statewide, that bring school teachers and higher education faculty together to share expertise and experience as they develop, validate, and replicate effective practices in science and mathematics teaching. Several concrete examples of successful K–16 professional learning communities are described. These examples include descriptions of how these K–16 professional learning communities were formed, how they overcame the most common barriers of time and communication, how the work evolved, and how the learning community impacted teaching and learning in both K–12 and higher education.

The chapter concludes with actions steps for K–16 educators and administrators on how to build K–16 professional learning communities at statewide, regional, and local levels, as well as methods for increasing the effectiveness of learning community facilitators and members. Particular attention is given to ways of growing a true sense of collegiality among K–12 and higher education faculty in order to increase the depth, impact, and sustainability of the professional learning community's work.

## DEFINING ELEMENTS OF PROFESSIONAL LEARNING COMMUNITIES

In professional learning communities, as defined by DuFour and Eaker (1998), all members are moving toward the same goal. The community, in support of moving toward that goal, collaborates to seek out best practices, implement and test best practices, and continually assess the impact. In Hord (1997), a professional learning community is defined as "a school in which the professionals (administrators and teachers) continuously seek and share learning to increase their effectiveness for students, and act on what they learn." Senge et al. (2000) define professional learning communities as "spaces" where people from different perspectives learn more powerfully in concert with others who are struggling with the same issues.

In Georgia, through the Partnership for Reform In Science and Mathematics (PRISM), professional learning communities have embraced these three perspectives while seeking to increase the impact of professional learning communities on student achievement in science and mathematics by involving participation of higher education faculty. The involvement of higher education science and mathematics faculty, college of education faculty, and K–12 teachers in K–16 professional learning communities strengthens the potential to bring concordance among strategies used in science and mathematics courses, those used in education pedagogy courses, and those teachers are taught to use in their K–12 classes.

PRISM professional learning communities bring K–12 teachers and higher education faculty together to share expertise and experience as they develop, validate, and replicate effective practices in science and mathematics teaching. It is from on-the-ground experience in building K–16 professional learning communities in science and mathematics that the reader is offered concrete strategies for building K–16 professional learning communities as an important component of your Science, Technology, Engineering, and Mathematics (STEM) Initiative.

## Defining K–16 Professional Learning Communities

In order to facilitate the development of K–16 professional learning communities in your state, it is important for your STEM leadership team to establish a set of defining elements (definition document) and a rubric for assessment. (See Appendix 6.1 for a copy of the rubric developed by PRISM.) Establishing these kinds of documents allows you to remain consistent with learning community definitions in the literature, while establishing, promoting, and assessing K–16 professional learning communities as they evolve.

As you develop your K–16 professional learning community definition document, a recommended focus is the trying, testing, verifying, and replicating of teaching practices deemed to have a positive impact on student learning in science and mathematics in K–12 schools, colleges, and universities. It is also important to build into it the needed flexibility that allows for autonomy and individuality of each professional learning community. Reaching agreement on a shared vision of teaching and learning among K–16 faculty participants should be a component of your definition document. The involvement of both K–12 and higher education faculty in K–16 professional learning communities is bedrock.

Another important component of your definition document of K–16 professional learning communities is leadership. In K–16 professional learning communities, leadership must be shared among teachers and college and university faculty, and they must be faculty-led. Another important consideration when developing your definition document is to include a statement that says K–16 professional learning communities commit to a set of values that build community and respect for diverse ideas and provide opportunities for K–16 educators to share what they know, consult with peers, and observe others at work. Finally, your work advances more quickly if your definition includes a statement that says K–16 professional learning communities are results-oriented and that learning community members engage in the process of collaborative inquiry. As an example, the PRISM definition document of K–16 professional learning communities in science and mathematics can be found in Appendix 6.2.

## Various Learning Community Models

Several viable and successful yet distinct implementation models, ranging from school-based professional learning communities to statewide communities of practice, can be created under the umbrella of your professional learning community definition. One model that works well is for professional learning communities to be school-based groups, organized by grade level and subject. Another model is for school-based professional learning communities to organize around a particular focus or theme, such as the development of integrated high school mathematics units or the investigation of inquiry-based teaching strategies in elementary school science.

School district-wide learning community constructs can also be established, including lead teacher professional learning communities that provide a collegial network for leaders of school-based professional learning communities. Multi-district or regional learning community structures can also be very successful. Several concrete examples of specific K–16 professional learning communities of each type can be found later in this chapter.

## CHARACTERISTICS AND IMPACT OF SUCCESSFUL STEM PROFESSIONAL LEARNING COMMUNITIES

There are at least three levels at which one might measure the success of a professional learning community. The long-term measure, and the ultimate goal of STEM professional learning communities, is increased student achievement. An intermediate measure and leading indicator of student success is improved practice of K–16 educators. A short-term measure is increased knowledge of the teachers or faculty. The potential of a learning community to achieve its goal is dependent upon the success of the learning community as an entity in itself.

In the late 1990s, Hord asserted that successful professional learning communities were characterized by five dimensions: shared leadership, shared vision, collective learning and application, supportive conditions, and shared practice (Hord 1997). Furthermore, these five dimensions serve as predictors of the impact of the professional learning community on student learning.

In a recent series of studies, Huffman and Hipp (2000) investigated the development of these characteristics in K–12 professional learning communities as well as the interdependence among these characteristics. Important initial steps to be taken by schools in order to build a thriving professional learning community characterized by strength in all five dimensions have also been put forth in the literature (Leo and Cowan 2000). From lessons learned in PRISM, the following attributes are added that are important for successful STEM K–16 professional learning communities.

## Leadership and Organization

Successful professional learning communities live within an atmosphere of shared leadership. Within such an atmosphere, the process of building a productive professional learning community is highly dependent upon an effective, energetic, and proactive facilitator or even better, a facilitation team. Successful school-level professional learning communities are frequently led by a lead teacher or instructional coach, chosen for his or her energy, experience, and leadership abilities. In district or regional-level professional learning communities, the facilitators are usually district curriculum coordinators and higher education faculty.

Although the leadership and decision-making of a well-functioning K–16 professional learning community is shared, the facilitator plays a particularly important role in establishing an environment for shared leadership. Facilitators organize meetings, deal with logistics, maintain open lines of communication with higher education participants, and often advocate for the needs of the professional learning community with K–12 administrators. Facilitators seek out resources and share information relevant to the work and focus of the professional learning community. In essence, the facilitator provides the framework upon which to build a productive and successful professional learning community.

## Professional Learning Focus

Successful STEM professional learning communities, functioning under the overarching goal of improving student achievement in science and mathematics, focus on data-driven teacher professional learning. The focus of a K–16 STEM learning community on science and mathematics content and pedagogy serves to coalesce a dichotomous group of K–16 educators into a true learning community. Learning-community-driven professional learning motivates collaboration through collective assessment of professional learning needs, analysis of student data, open discussions of areas of weakness, and sharing of instructional strengths.

The K–16 collaborative environment supports professional learning that clearly connects science and mathematics content knowledge, pedagogical theory, and classroom practice. The K–16 professional learning community provides a forum for discussion of classroom effectiveness and use of knowledge gained as teachers implement and fine tune classroom instruction based on new learning. Learning-community-driven professional learning is ongoing as additional needs arise from new student data and ongoing implementation.

## Process of Development

While professional learning communities mature at drastically different rates depending upon many factors, there is still a common process of development for STEM K–16 professional learning communities. The initial task is to assess professional learning needs. Methods of assessment include teacher self-assessment surveys, analysis of standardized test scores, review of student work samples, and student grades on teacher-made assignments.

From these data, professional learning community members work to meet teacher professional learning needs through a collaborative planning and delivery process. Teachers engaging in the learning activities begin to collaboratively plan lesson plans and units. Teachers share resources and present successful strategies for implementing the knowledge gained in professional learning experiences.

As the learning community matures further, peer observation is used to assess classroom impact and also to lay the groundwork for shared practice. K–16 professional learning communities advance with the design and implementation of action research projects, engaging in more collective inquiry. In the most advanced stages, K–16 professional learning communities engage in successful implementation of research, and collaborations expand even further to include grant writing, community outreach, and many forms of dissemination of classroom impact.

## Higher Education Faculty Participation

The depth of involvement of higher education faculty in K–16 professional learning communities is an evolving entity. STEM faculty have the potential to contribute not only depth of content knowledge but also high levels of enthusiasm for science and mathematics as well as experience in scientific inquiry. While education faculty have much more experience in partnering with K–12 schools, STEM faculty bring varying degrees of prior engagement with K–12 education.

The initial task of a STEM faculty member newly engaged with K–12 is to become familiar with K–12 teachers, their practices, their culture, and also the content and flow of the K–12 curriculum. Establishing truly equitable and collegial relationships is absolutely necessary to sustainable participation in the learning community.

A successfully maturing relationship between higher education faculty and K–12 teachers can be described as appreciative and respectful. It is one where teachers are comfortable expressing content weaknesses and professional learning needs and relying on the higher education faculty to understand and fulfill those areas of need. It is one where higher education faculty have witnessed firsthand the overwhelmingly hectic lives of K–12 teachers and are determined to find an avenue for making a valuable contribution to teaching and learning in K–12 schools.

Once inspired by this realization of how STEM faculty might fulfill a significant K–12 need, particularly one that focused on professional learning, the level of collaboration increases quite rapidly. This stage of collaboration empowers teachers to design their own professional learning. The level of collegiality among K–16 educators is high. Indeed, learning-community-driven professional learning engages K–16 educators in collaboration and collective learning as they analyze student data and design, deliver, and assess classroom impact.

A significant investment of time into the task of collaboratively designed content-based professional learning often brings with it a heightened level of cooperation, one that is characterized by truly equitable relationships and activities that take on the nature of shared practice and classroom experimentation. Many K–16 collaborations initiated through collaborative design of professional learning have grown into team teaching experiments and collaborative action research projects.

## Impact on Teaching and Learning

The fact that professional learning community participation leads to enhanced K–16 teaching and learning is undeniable. Outcomes that can be attributed to PRISM professional learning communities include improved classroom practice, increased student achievement, increased participation of K–16 educators in quality professional learning, and increased involvement of faculty in educational research and the scholarship of teaching and learning.

*Impact on K–12.* The most transparent outcome of learning community participation for K–12 teachers is improved classroom practice. One hundred percent of PRISM participants from K–12 schools indicate the use of new strategies, materials, or assessments as a result of professional learning community participation. New strategies implemented include hands-on and inquiry-based teaching methods and cooperative learning strategies. New materials and assessments used, such as manipulatives and performance assessments, complement the new strategies implemented.

K–12 teachers have also increased the use of appropriate technology in the classroom and they spend more time involving students in laboratory experiments.

There is also evidence that the higher education presence increases the classroom impact of the professional learning community. Learning-community-driven professional learning significantly deepens the ability to transfer increased content knowledge to the classroom and creates the avenue for improving and fine tuning classroom instruction as it is delivered. Furthermore, teachers in professional learning communities with higher education STEM faculty members are using more standards-based and inquiry-based instruction than teachers in professional learning communities without a strong connection to higher education.

While it is difficult to provide firm evidence of cause, teachers also assert that there are numerous indicators of increased student learning resulting from improvements in instruction that can be attributed to learning community participation. These indicators include increased standardized test scores, improved performance on teacher-made classroom assessments, increased levels of student participation and homework completion, positive feedback from parents, and increased student interest in science and mathematics classroom activities. Indeed, a significant majority of K–12 participants cite benefits to students as the most positive outcome of their professional learning community participation.

***Impact on Higher Education.***    The benefit most often cited by higher education members of professional learning communities is the inspiration to try new classroom strategies and assessments in their college-level courses. Classroom changes cited include reducing classroom lectures and increasing field experiences, increasing student involvement and participation, increased use of inquiry and group work, and experimenting with alternative formative assessments to guide instruction.

In many cases, these changes have materialized into the development of classroom research and experimentation. Indeed, participation in educational research and scholarship of teaching and learning has risen significantly for higher education professional learning community participants. Activities range from actions taken to become more knowledgeable about the scholarship of teaching and learning to dissemination of educational research results. This increased use of inquiry-based and student-centered teaching and learning strategies by higher education faculty has resulted in decreased student withdrawal rates and increased passing rates in introductory science and mathematics courses at all four participating PRISM Georgia institutions.

# CONDITIONS FOR PROFESSIONAL LEARNING COMMUNITY SUCCESS

K–16 professional learning communities can be a highly effective strategy in a comprehensive STEM Initiative in your state or region. To ensure their effectiveness, putting in place the following conditions is recommended.

## Support of a STEM Partnership

The support and advocacy that can be provided through a well-established K–16 partnership including key stakeholders in K–16 education has significant impact on the success of K–16 professional learning communities. These partnerships play an integral role in building the conditions for K–16 professional learning communities to thrive, including holding the power to embed the work of K–16 professional learning communities and the associated outcomes into the workload and professional expectations of K–16 educators.

State, school, and university administrators are in positions to provide needed support for teachers and higher education faculty to collaborate in K–16 professional learning communities. K–12 administrators can provide incentives for Lead Teachers to participate and advocate for time to be built into the school day for teachers to gather in professional learning communities. Higher education administrators can provide leadership in changing the faculty reward system to one that rewards and promotes higher education faculty for significant work in K–12 schools.

K–16 partnerships also have the potential to promote the benefits of professional learning communities throughout school districts and higher education institutions. Good partnerships should model best practices for budding K–16 professional learning communities. An established educational partnership also provides an avenue for sustaining the quality of the work through changes in school or university personnel and even statewide legislations. Attributes of effective K–16 partnerships and the potential of partnerships to serve as avenues for improving K–16 STEM teaching and learning are given in chapter 2.

## Organization by a Collaborative K–16 Team

A highly collaborative coordination team, involving at least one representative from K–12 and one representative from higher education, is important to establishing effective K–16 professional learning communities.

The higher education coordinator should bring a collegial relationship with K–12 schools. He or she should also be an integral and respected member of the higher education STEM community. This person should be able to advocate for the value of the higher education contribution to K–12 schools. The higher education team member can help other STEM faculty find a good connection to K–12 needs.

The K–12 coordinator should enjoy a good relationship with higher education faculty and be a highly respected member of the K–12 community. His or her role would also include helping make connections between higher education faculty and K–12 needs. This coordination team bears the responsibility of facilitating relationships, providing organizational structures, finding resources, and maintaining an active and open network of communication.

Taking time to build the support for STEM K–16 professional learning communities pays huge dividends in being able to inspire and recruit teachers and higher education faculty. The following important contacts are recommended: Teachers, principals, district administrators, higher education faculty, department heads, deans, and vice presidents. One cannot overemphasize the importance of clear and frequent communication in any newly established program, particularly one where success depends upon the blending of two fairly dichotomous cultures (K–12 and higher education). The engagement of higher education faculty in professional learning communities with teachers requires personal contacts from the very beginning and requires ongoing attention.

## Training for Facilitators and Participants

Even in a district or region where schools and higher education institutions are at very high levels of readiness to engage in professional learning communities, training designed for STEM learning community facilitators and participants is invaluable. It is especially important in the most common situation where classroom teachers serve as learning community leaders and STEM faculty with little previous connection to K–12 schools are participating in school-based professional learning communities.

Clarifying roles, potential contributions, and outlining steps that can be taken to become more effective learning community members greatly accelerates the development of STEM K–16 professional learning communities. Existing programs such as Critical Friends or Whole Faculty Study Groups (Murphey and Lick 2005) provide a variety of protocols for engaging educators in professional learning communities. PRISM partners developed and provided a Lead Teacher Academy to prepare teacher leaders to implement and facilitate school-level professional learning communities across the state.

*Example: Agenda for Lead Teacher Academy.* Effective Leadership for Science and Mathematics Workshop Outcomes:

- Learn about effective leadership practices, especially those influencing student achievement in science and mathematics
- Understand the components of PRISM
- Understand the job responsibilities of a PRISM Lead Teacher
- Network with PRISM staff and fellow teacher leaders

Day 1:

| | |
|---|---|
| 10:00am–10:15am | Self-Assessment Activity |
| 10:15am–11:15am | Welcome, Introductions, and Goals for Today |
| 11:15am–12:00pm | PRISM Overview |
| 12:00pm–1:00pm | Lunch |
| 1:00pm–3:00pm | Leading Every Day: Effective Leadership Practices |
| 3:00pm–3:15pm | Break |
| 3:15pm–3:45pm | Leadership Practices Inventory |
| 3:45pm–4:00 pm | Closing Remarks |
| 4:00pm–5:00 pm | Regional Plans and Reflections |

Day 2:

| | |
|---|---|
| 8:00am–8:15am | Self-Assessment Activity |
| 8:15am–8:30am | Introductions, Overview, and Goals for Today |
| 8:30am–10:00am | Letting Data Lead the Way to Improved Student Achievement in Science and Mathematics |
| 10:00am–10:15am | Break |
| 10:15am–12:00pm | Effectively Leading Professional Learning in Science and Mathematics |
| 12:00pm–12:15pm | Closing Remarks |

Annual learning community workshops are also recommended to provide tools, guidance, and opportunities for K–12 teachers and higher education faculty to engage in initial planning for professional learning communities.

## Valued Outcomes for K–12 Teachers and Higher Education Faculty

In order to truly succeed in creating viable and sustainable K–16 professional learning communities, the potential outcomes of the work need to be valued not only by the participants but also by K–12 and higher education administrations. The impetus for implementing K–16 professional learning communities as an avenue for increases in student achievement certainly provides initial motivation for participation. It may also create advocates in administration, gain the interest of the media, and elicit some level of support from the community. Nonetheless, these benefits are not sustainable if professional learning communities do not produce outcomes and products that are in line with the professional expectations of the STEM educators involved.

The time spent in professional learning communities is more productive if it is not an add-on to the already full workload of the teachers and faculty. The work of a STEM learning community should blend well into K–12 and higher education cultures. In PRISM professional learning communities, teachers earned professional learning units for their participation and many facilitators earned the position of academic coach or instructional lead teacher. Through PRISM, the University System of Georgia also changed its policy to one of advocacy for contributions of all higher education faculty to K–12 schools (for more detail, see chapter 7).

### Supportive Conditions

A final and simply stated condition for success is the existence of supportive conditions within schools and higher education departments. Time and scheduling is a big issue. Sparks (2002) insists, "Time must be built into the school day and year." In a K–16 STEM learning community, it is difficult for K–12 teachers and higher education faculty to achieve true egalitarianism without spending a significant amount of time together, in person, creating a sense of community. Given this, it is equally important for departments to find ways to be flexible with faculty schedules allowing them enough time to fully participate in school-based professional learning communities.

## EXAMPLES OF MODEL PROFESSIONAL LEARNING COMMUNITIES

Several concrete descriptions of successful K–16 professional learning communities follow. Each example includes descriptions of how the learning community was formed, how the group overcame barriers as they presented themselves, how the work evolved, and how the learning community impacted teaching and learning of science and mathematics at the K–12 and/or the higher education level.

## School- or Institution-Level Professional Learning Communities

*Southwest Elementary School Learning Community.* The Southwest Elementary School Learning Community was initiated as a result of the principal's interest in participating in a regional Math-Science Partnership program. The school could be characterized as having a low to medium level of readiness to implement professional learning communities. There was little flexibility in scheduling to allow teachers to meet during the school day. Teachers met frequently, yet informally, to plan instruction collaboratively. Prior to PRISM, the school lacked a formal teacher leadership presence. The connection to higher education had been minimal and teachers rarely went beyond what was required when using data to guide instruction. Due to the advocacy of the principal and the energy of the lead teacher, this school now has a thriving and successful K–16 STEM learning community.

In 2003, the Southwest Elementary School PRISM Learning Community was implemented. Participation is fully voluntary and yet twenty of the thirty-nine regular teachers participate in the meetings that occur once per month after school. There are four higher education STEM faculty who are regular members of the Southwest Elementary School Learning Community and have not only participated in the analysis of student data but have also studied the elementary school performance standards and curriculum at length.

The primary activity of this learning community has consistently been to work closely with the higher education members to plan professional learning collaboratively in reaction to weaknesses in student achievement. Each year, the professional learning focus and corresponding activities have shifted based upon standardized test scores from the previous year. The focus of the first year was problem solving in mathematics. In the second year, the learning community focused on weather, geology, and the environment.

Each of these years culminated in increased student achievement on standardized tests in these areas. Indeed, the percent of students meeting or exceeding standards on the state-normed mathematics exam increased by an average of 7 percent across all grades at Southwest Elementary School. The K–16 relationships forged through the collaborative development of professional learning in this learning community have resulted in new university courses for elementary school teachers and presentations at national meetings co-presented by a K–12 and higher education team.

*Metter High School Science Learning Community.* The Metter High School Science Learning Community has been in existence for four years. It began when three high school science teachers began working with and understanding the new state science standards. Many of the new performance standard tasks required the use of Computer-Based Laboratory (CBL) technology. The teachers were neither familiar with CBL technology nor with how to incorporate it into their classrooms. The teachers reached out to Georgia Southern University for help and PRISM partners established a link with the chemistry department.

A chemistry professor invited the high school science teachers to the university to look at the available CBL technology. He offered to create a class that would show them how to use the technology. They began meeting monthly in 2004 to outline the course and write a grant to support their work. Face-to-face meetings and e-mail communication were frequent. Much study was done with the CBL technology and incorporating it into inquiry science lessons. More teachers and more college professors became involved as the work developed.

The CBL technology was integrated into the classrooms in the 2005–2006 school year. The teachers continue to learn new technology together and continue to develop new inquiry lessons. The professors visit and observe the lessons in action and offer support and guidance. In 2007–2008, the K–16 professional learning community has instructed the middle and elementary teachers in this school district on the use of this technology. By the end of 2008, science instruction at all levels within the school district included CBL technology.

The research has shown that the students prefer to use the CBL equipment over traditional equipment in terms of interest, accuracy, precision, and perceived quality of data. Traditional equipment is still considered easier to use. During this time of development and implementation, the school has experienced sizable gains in standardized science test scores.

## District-Level and Regional Professional Learning Communities

*The Northeast Georgia Regional AP Calculus Learning Community.* The Northeast Georgia AP Calculus Learning Community was initiated and supported through the implementation of PRISM. Nineteen AP Calculus high school teachers from twelve school districts traveled during the work week to meet in their professional learning community for several hours each month. The goal of this community was to help students excel in AP Calculus and ultimately earn exemplary scores on the College Board by deepening their content knowledge and broadening their instructional expertise.

Teachers worked toward this goal by sharing successful lessons, working together to develop strategies to motivate students, and discussing review techniques. The higher education faculty presence is strong in this professional learning community. The group is facilitated by a University of Georgia (UGA) faculty member and also has a UGA mathematician who is a full-fledged member of the community.

While the K–12 teachers are truly the leaders in this community, the emergence and strengthening of this group as a thriving regional learning community is largely due to the higher education facilitator. The AP Calculus learning community facilitator was an experienced high school AP Calculus teacher, well versed in team-building skills, protocols for establishing shared vision and leadership, and using data to drive and assess progress and effectiveness of the learning community.

Initial tasks included team-building activities and this initial investment of time spent building a sense of community was certainly worthwhile. After only a few meetings, all teachers were sharing lesson plans and discussing areas of weakness. In between meetings, teachers in this community contacted each other regularly to exchange ideas and resources. They were very comfortable calling on the higher education participants for help.

The UGA Mathematics professor often worked with a subset of the teachers on Calculus BC topics as well as led whole-group discussions upon request. However, he was most often just one more voice around the table as the group worked together to deepen their conceptual knowledge.

After only one year, there was dramatic evidence of increased student achievement. The number of students taking the AP Calculus test increased by 10 percent across the AP classes of the learning community members. The most emphatic evidence of the impact of this learning community is the percent of students passing the AP Calculus text. After only one full year of implementation, the percent of students passing the AP test increased by over 20 percent for the learning community teachers while the state of Georgia only increased by 1 percent and the national percentage remained unchanged.

***Glynn County Elementary School Inquiry in Science Learning Community.*** The Glynn County Elementary School Inquiry in Science Learning Community began in the fall of 2005. This group is composed of several instructional coaches and twenty teachers from five elementary schools in Glynn County as well as a number of science faculty members from Coastal Georgia Community College. The facilitator of this community is an elementary education faculty member from Armstrong Atlantic State University.

Test score analysis and teacher surveys revealed a need for a professional learning focus on inquiry methods and physical science with a particular emphasis on third- and fourth-grade content standards. For three years, this learning community has been implementing an ongoing project with the primary goal being to raise third- and fourth-grade student achievement scores in physical science through increased use of the inquiry method.

The work of this learning community began with several half-day Saturday sessions at each school as well as at the college. They examined the literature and the resource rooms to become more familiar with inquiry research and to determine what materials were already available for use in designing inquiry-based lessons. While digging through resources, the teachers and higher education faculty produced a more-detailed outline of professional learning content.

The learning community engaged in several full-day professional learning sessions interspersed throughout the year, each involving a particular physical science content and related inquiry strategies. Teachers collaborate in writing the unit objectives in alignment with the Georgia Performance Standards. Between learning sessions, participants implement the units involving pre-service elementary education majors as teaching assistants and are observed by other members of the learning community. The learning community still meets to discuss effectiveness of classroom implementation, fine tune lesson plans, and prepare for the next iteration of content.

In the first year, students given a pre-test and post-test on content showed an average gain of 13.1 percent across all participating Glynn County elementary schools. This learning community has not only improved science instruction in Glynn county elementary schools, but it has also greatly enhanced the value of the pre-service practicum experience for the region's future teachers.

***Southeast Georgia PRISM Learning Community.*** What began as a collaborative method of coordinating regional implementation of PRISM soon evolved into a true K–16 learning community. This monthly gathering of over 100 learning community participants includes eighty K–12 teachers, who are also facilitators of PRISM school-based professional learning communities, and over forty higher education faculty members of school-based PRISM professional learning communities.

The initial role of this group was to provide information and support to the newly established K–16 professional learning communities in the region. Meetings were structured around participant presentations and small group sharing sessions. This group developed collaboratively a regional professional learning agenda based upon multi-district data aggregated by grade level. School learning community facilitators shared successes and struggles.

In the next stage of development, the group engaged much more frequently in collective learning. Topics studied from a variety of perspectives included interdisciplinary teaching and curricula, performance-based assessment, and inquiry-based teaching and learning. The region has observed that professional learning communities draw strength from the existence of a network of professional learning communities including a very active regional learning community at the center.

The Southeast regional learning community provides leadership, guidance, and opportunities with the goal of facilitating the work of the school professional learning communities. This opportunity for learning community leaders to share ideas and learn from each other has impacted the development of PRISM professional learning communities relative to the PRISM K–16 professional learning community defining elements, mentioned previously. In only a few short years, this regional learning community has inspired over 110 professional learning activities, generated ideas for twenty or more educational research projects, and supported the implementation of 171 school-based professional learning communities across four school districts.

***Northeast Georgia Mathematics Curriculum Team.***   The PRISM Mathematics Curriculum Team was created in the spring of 2006 at the University of Georgia (UGA) to review and revise UGA courses for prospective mathematics teachers to reflect the new Georgia Performance Standards (GPS). Educators from mathematics and mathematics education at UGA who had particular skills and training were recruited to study collaboratively the new standards and create units of instruction that offer pre-service teachers training in an integrated standards-based approach to teaching mathematics. They were joined by a middle school teacher and a high school teacher who each had been working on GPS materials for their school districts.

These teachers took the lead in helping the UGA members understand what the state is requiring of teachers as the change is made to the GPS. The team soon realized the need for a statistician to help with the data analysis strand in the standards and invited a faculty member from the UGA department of statistics to join the group. The team currently is composed of seven UGA professors—three mathematicians, two statisticians, and two mathematics educators—a middle school teacher and a high school teacher, and a facilitator. The main activities of the Mathematics Curriculum Team include (1) developing units of instruction for UGA courses and (2) sharing the vision of the new state curriculum with colleagues and others.

In developing units, the team has found that they focus on important mathematics and emphasize the big ideas. They naturally integrate mathematics in a meaningful way. The Georgia Performance Standards have embraced the importance of statistical reasoning across the K–12 curriculum, so the team explored the inclusion of data analysis in the units of instruction. There have been many discussions between the statisticians and mathematicians on the team about the difference between mathematical and statistical thinking. One of the benefits of teaching statistics and mathematics together is that statistics can enliven a class through real-life examples that motivate and illustrate virtually any topic in school mathematics.

The PRISM Mathematics Curriculum Team presented their work to more than 100 mathematics educators at the annual conference of the National Council of Teachers of Mathematics in March 2007. The team also shared the standards and the work with their own colleagues back at the University of Georgia through a series of collegial luncheons. In addition to reaching out to UGA colleagues, the PRISM Mathematics Curriculum Team has given several presentations at national and regional conferences.

## Statewide Professional Learning Communities

*Georgia's Institute for Teaching and Learning of Science and Mathematics.* A principal strategy of PRISM is to influence the quality of instruction in higher education mathematics and science courses, particularly those at the introductory level. Success within this strategy benefits future teachers by providing models of quality instruction in science and mathematics. Improved instruction in high school and higher education also increases overall success rates in core science and mathematics courses that in turn should increase the number of students choosing or at least maintaining science or mathematics as a major field of study.

PRISM partners established a statewide learning community involving hundreds of high school science and mathematics teachers and higher education STEM faculty working together toward these goals. This learning community is structured as a network where a core group of 80 to 100 members meet twice annually at a statewide institute. Participants attend in teams of representatives from regional institutes from across the state. These regional institutes also have the form of professional learning communities and complement the statewide institute in many ways.

These two-day institutes involve plenary speakers on recent topics in scholarly teaching and learning, with particular relevance to mathematics and science. Plenary speakers have engaged this large community in collective learning about such topics as student misconceptions in science and mathematics, inquiry-based teaching and learning, intelligence and complex reasoning, and assessment in science and mathematics instruction. The institutes involve discipline-focused sessions that provide cross-regional networking and sharing time among institute members from various system institutions.

Additionally, in stark contrast with professional conferences, the institutes provide ample time for team reflection and regional institute planning. Indeed, throughout the year, the regional institute members engage in a variety of activities in which they further investigate and apply the topics introduced at the statewide institutes.

Supporting structures for this continued work at the institutional level include smaller-scale replicas of the state-level meetings involving redelivery of topics investigated at the state level, scholarly roundtable discussions, collective reviews of the literature, small grants for classroom experimentation, and other efforts to improve instruction. These regional activities expand the opportunities for sharing, collective learning, and reflection on scholarly teaching topics to the broader group of science and mathematics teachers and STEM faculty in the region.

Evidence is emerging that classroom strategies implemented as a result of the PRISM Institute are having a positive effect of student achievement. As an example, a cross-institutional team of institute faculty experimenting with "studio physics," a collegiate inquiry-based integration of lecture and laboratory work, has shown significant reductions in student failure rates as well as an overall increase in student persistence in physics. Additionally, the six higher education institutions participating in the PRISM Institute since 2003 have shown greater increases in student success in introductory mathematics courses between 2003 and 2006 than the university system taken as a whole.

## ACTION STEPS FOR K–16 EDUCATORS AND ADMINISTRATORS

K–16 professional learning communities are proving to be a very strong strategy for improving teaching and learning in science and mathematics in both schools and colleges. Their inclusion in the design of the STEM initiative in your state is highly recommended. The following steps are intended to offer guidance as you build K–16 professional learning communities:

- Use an existing and strong K–16 partnership, if possible, to obtain a solid base support for the implementation and facilitation of professional learning communities from both school districts and higher education administrators.

- Implement, if feasible, a network of professional learning communities involving several schools and higher education institutions working toward a common overarching goal, but maintaining autonomy to focus individual learning community work on specific needs. The central learning community in this network should provide an avenue for sharing and learning across all learning communities.
- Establish a highly collaborative regional team with representation from both higher education and K–12 schools, to provide support to learning community facilitators, enhance communication, and coordinate learning community efforts at a regional level. This team should also be an ongoing resource for both K–16 professional learning communities and their individual members.
- Provide high-quality training for professional learning community facilitators and participants. Not everyone knows how to be a good partner.
- Involve significant numbers of K–12 teachers and higher education faculty in designing the regional implementation plans and activities. The involvement of a critical mass of participants in the developmental stages of the partnership allows for participant ownership of the learning community structure and activities. This will greatly increase motivation of participants and ultimately increase the productivity and impact of your professional learning communities.
- Determine collectively how success will be measured and share and assess progress regularly as a group.
- Make available structured opportunities for K–16 professional learning communities to engage in collective learning, true collaboration, and shared practice. These opportunities should be true learning experiences for both K–12 teachers and higher education faculty.
- Provide venues to publicly celebrate and showcase success and impact of learning community work.
- Ensure that the work of the learning community members, both K–12 and higher education, is recognized, valued, and counted toward professional enhancement and advancement.

## NOTE

1. Sabrina A. Hessinger is a regional co-principal investigator in the Partnership for Reform In Science and Mathematics (PRISM), a systemic K–16 STEM initiative in Georgia. She is an associate professor of mathematics and Special Assistant to the Dean of the College of Science and Technology in charge of the STEM Initiative at Armstrong Atlantic State University in Savannah.

**7**

# ENGAGING HIGHER EDUCATION FACULTY IN K–16 STEM EDUCATION REFORM

*Charles Kutal, Frederick Rich, Sabrina A. Hessinger,*
*and H. Richard Miller*[1]

## INTRODUCTION

Much has been written about the importance of school-college (K–16) partnerships to support a smoother transition for students from high school to college. Likewise, much has been written about the need for K–16 partnerships to prepare and support the transition of teachers from higher education (where they are prepared) to the schools, where they are assigned to teach. Chapters 1 and 2 of this book add further to the reasons for K–16 partnerships when states are attempting to launch systemic reform initiatives in science, technology, engineering, and mathematics (STEM) that result in improved student achievement in mathematics and in the sciences.

What has been written about less frequently is how to go about interesting and engaging higher education faculty to partner with K–12 in STEM initiatives. In teacher preparation programs there is a rich history of school-college collaboration, but it has largely been between colleges of education and the schools. While these two partners are critical to increasing student learning and achievement in science and mathematics, there has often been a missing partner—STEM faculty.

If you already have established K–16 partnerships in place with rich collaboration among higher education faculty (colleges of arts and sciences and education), K–12 school teachers, and officials in state education agencies, then, as noted in chapter 2, you are well on your way. With these partnerships in place you are well-positioned to build on them when launching your K–16 STEM initiative.

But what if you do not have K–16 partnerships in place? Chapter 2 offers many tips on how to build partnerships. This chapter focuses on concrete strategies you can put in place to really engage STEM higher education faculty in your work to increase student learning and achievement in these fields in both schools and colleges. A central principle of the NSF Math and Science Partnership program is that without real buy-in of STEM faculty, it is not possible to break the cycle of low student interest, achievement, and preparedness for careers in science, technology, engineering, and mathematics.

## HOW TO BEGIN

While the need for K–12 education reform is widely accepted (Business-Higher Education Forum 2005; Project Kaleidoscope 2006), most higher education faculty members are reluctant to participate owing to the lack of professional recognition and tangible rewards (Gips 1998; Zhang et al. 2007). In other words, they get rewarded through such things as promotion, tenure, and salary increases for other kinds of work—largely their teaching and their research. So it is important, early on in your STEM initiative, to include a strategy focused on changing the reward system for higher education faculty so that their interest in K–16 STEM reform can change to commitment for their long-term participation.

In the design of the Partnership for Reform In Science and Mathematics (PRISM) in Georgia, our specific strategy was to provide a reward structure in universities to encourage faculty members to sustain involvement in improving STEM teaching and learning in K–12 schools. Our recommendations in this chapter come from lived experience in trying to succeed with this strategy in the University System of Georgia (USG)—a system of thirty-five public colleges and universities. For details on the process followed in creating a new higher education reward structure in Georgia, see Kozaitis (2008), Kutal et al. (2006), and Rich et al. (2007).

### Putting a Structure in Place

When trying to change the higher education faculty reward system in your state, it is important to have broad-based participation of faculty and those with positional authority over implementation of the reward system. For example, disciplinary faculty in each department, the department chairs, and college deans currently have important roles in implementing the faculty reward system within each university. If each college or university is part of a university system—as is the case in Georgia—then academic leaders from the university system office must also be involved. Some kind of structure is needed that brings all of these voices to the table and engages all participants fully in the redesign of the faculty reward system.

An initial decision you must make is—who leads this strategy? In chapter 2, an important point was made about "sharing leadership" in your K–16 STEM initiative. This means that the K–12 and higher education communities share leadership for the overall initiative. But, at the strategy level, the leader should be the person with the greatest credibility to accomplish that strategy. The strategy about changing the higher education faculty reward system should be led by an individual from higher education with the clout to get the job done and strong credibility with higher education faculty.

Even with this individual identified, it is important to take a committee approach to this strategy. A group of faculty leaders—in this case from STEM fields and colleges of education, along with a few key department chairs, deans, and, if applicable, university system office academic leaders—form the committee. You may also want to include a cultural anthropologist on the committee—since success in this particular strategy includes changing both policies and practices (institutional culture).

The leader of the committee then becomes the facilitator. The committee collaboratively develops the overall plan for how to go about achieving this strategy. A cultural anthropologist, if involved, can help you study the process of change to see if your work is taking root among faculty members and chairs in academic departments throughout one or more colleges and universities. If change does not happen among academic departments, all effort to change the higher education faculty reward system is not sustainable.

## Creating a Process for Large-Scale Faculty Involvement

With your committee in place for this strategy—to change the higher education faculty reward system—an important step is to figure out how to involve large numbers of faculty, department chairs, and deans in the process. One way to do this is to develop reflection questions on: (1) factors leading to student underachievement in STEM disciplines; (2) potential alliances between higher education and K–12 schools to improve STEM education; (3) barriers to, and strategies for, productive STEM partnerships; and (4) incentives and rewards that would encourage higher education faculty to help improve STEM education.

Using such questions—perhaps in focus groups—your committee could seek broad-based views of all stakeholders before it designs specific tactics to achieve this strategy. The anthropologist on your committee could then conduct an ethnographic analysis to determine core themes within and across each category of participants.

With such core themes identified, it is important to bring together a large group of STEM faculty, department chairs, and deans, along with their counterparts in colleges of education. An event, such as a symposium, could help you to translate broad-based themes into something more concrete. For example, you could use a structured qualitative instrument to elicit input on: (1) activities related to engagement in K–12 schools that faculty may incorporate into a preexisting academic workload in the categories of research, instruction, and service; and (2) incentives and rewards that would encourage sustainable participation by higher education faculty and students to participate in the improvement of K–16 mathematics and science education.

The purpose of such a symposium is to continue the dialogue with the participants in the exploratory phase of work on this strategy, and to extend the conversation to a larger number of faculty and administrators from additional departments, colleges, and institutions. To ensure that your work plan for this strategy includes the views of all key stakeholders, you could organize the responses to the questions on the structured qualitative instrument into the following categories: (1) academic discipline (e.g., mathematics, science, engineering, education); (2) professional title (e.g., chair, dean, provost); (3) academic rank (e.g., assistant, associate, full professor); and (4) sector (e.g., research university, community college), if you are seeking change throughout a university system of multiple institutions.

If your analysis of participant responses mirrors that found in Georgia, faculty rewards are likely viewed differently by groups depending on their faculty rank, tenure status, and institutional sector. Nonetheless, cutting across all groups, your participants are likely to recommend a reward structure comprised of time release, workload reduction, salary increase, summer salary, and credit toward promotion and tenure. While priority of these rewards may vary according to rank, your faculty and administrators from each sector, institution, and discipline are likely to agree that such rewards are necessary to encourage, increase, and sustain involvement in K–16 STEM education reform.

Gathering and analyzing information of this type from a broad cross-section of higher education faculty and administrators is an important step that should be followed in the design of your strategy to change the higher education faculty reward system. At a very basic level, such information may help you see that you don't have all needed players on your committee.

Development of an Implementation Framework (see example in Appendix 7.1) may help your committee to ensure it is addressing sustainable change in different organizational contexts. The Framework, then, can be used to guide plans to change both policy and practice at four levels: system, institution, college, and department. The recognition that this change in the culture of higher education must be embraced at all of these levels should guide the strategic thinking of your committee.

If you are seeking to change both policy and practice at all four of these levels within your Implementation Framework, it is important for committee members to review the promotion and tenure policies of their own institutions as they relate to faculty working with K–12 schools. Such an analysis is likely to show that existing policies do not prohibit such involvement. Most current policies just don't encourage it or advocate for it.

So again, an important step is to take the conversations deeper within multiple parts of a single university or, if a university system is involved, within several colleges and universities. Feedback from these meetings is likely to demonstrate that there is no one single course of action applicable to all institutions. Changes in policy and practice that encourage greater participation of higher education faculty in K–16 STEM education reform must recognize the differences in mission and faculty workloads among the various departments, colleges, and institutions.

## CHANGES IN STATE-LEVEL POLICY

If a university system of multiple higher education institutions is part of your STEM initiative, development of system-level policy is desirable. For example, in Georgia, thirty-five public higher education institutions are part of the University System of Georgia that is governed by a single governing board—the Board of Regents. This phenomenon made it critical for us to develop and then to seek adoption of a new policy at the Board of Regents level.

Since our motivation in Georgia was to change the faculty reward system so that collaboration with K–12 schools was valued, our new policy is called a *Work in the Schools* policy (see below). This policy specifically advocates rewarding faculty for working with K–12 schools, for improving their own teaching, and for contributing scholarship that promotes and improves student performance. Importantly, it provides the umbrella for institutions to use in developing similar policies or procedures at the institutional, college, and departmental levels. The policy has the flexibility to encompass all types of universities and local department values in decision-making for promotion and tenure, as well as a continuum of definitions of scholarship. It was adopted by the Board of Regents in October 2006 and applies to all thirty-five institutions in the University System of Georgia.

*University System of Georgia Board of Regents Policy Statement 803.17 Work in the Schools.* Board of Regents' approval of University System of Georgia institutions to prepare teachers includes the expectation that state colleges and universities with a teacher preparation mission will collaborate with the K–12 schools. University System institutions that prepare teachers will support and reward all faculty who participate significantly in teacher preparation and in school improvement efforts through decisions in promotion and tenure, pre-tenure and post-tenure review, annual review and merit pay, workload, recognition, allocation of resources, and other rewards. Participation in teacher preparation and in school improvement may include documented efforts of these faculty in:

- Improving their own teaching so as to model effective teaching practices in courses taken by prospective teachers.
- Contributing scholarship that promotes and improves student learning and achievement in the schools and in the university.
- Collaborating with public schools to strengthen teaching quality and to increase student learning.

The chancellor shall issue guidelines, to be published in the Academic Affairs Handbook, that serve to encourage formal institutional recognition and reward for all faculty in realizing the expectations embodied in this policy.

## Using Change in Policy to Bring About Changes in Practice

Using Georgia's policy as an example, the last sentence in the above statement triggers an important next phase of work for your committee that is overseeing the work to change the faculty reward system in your STEM initiative. A very necessary next step is development of guidelines for implementation of the new policy.

Our guidelines charge each president with implementation of the new policy at the institutional level where he or she is responsible for providing leadership for advocating, assessing, and rewarding practices. The guidelines address sustainability with a variety of incentives (see Appendix 7.2 for University System of Georgia's Guidelines).

Once guidelines for implementation are completed, a next recommended step is creation of a dedicated Web site for faculty to get common definitions, examples of evidence, and case study exemplars for the following activities involving faculty work in the schools: scholarly teaching; scholarship of discovery; engagement and teaching and learning; and service (see Appendix 7.3).

## CHANGES IN INSTITUTIONAL-LEVEL POLICY

If a university system is involved in your STEM partnership, policy change at the state-level is only part of what is needed. Policy changes at the level of each college and university may also be needed. One or more of the colleges or universities in your STEM initiative may already be reevaluating its faculty roles and reward structure. If so, you are likely to find that creation of a new state-level policy, such as the *Work in the Schools* policy in the University System of Georgia, can be used to accelerate the process at institutions where work is already underway.

For example, such colleges or universities may modify their promotion and tenure policies to advocate for faculty involvement in K–16 educational reform. You could see statements like the following begin to appear in university-level policies: "Frequency and quality of interaction with school teachers" and "development of materials that maximize student learning" can be counted toward promotion and tenure.

At other universities, you may find those who have already accepted as valuable faculty work in what is called the "scholarship of teaching and learning." In these universities, you are likely to find that adoption of a state-level policy such as *Work in the Schools* is rather quickly being replicated in institutional, college, and departmental promotion and tenure policies.

At still other universities, you may find that institutional-level promotion and tenure policies don't necessarily follow a change at the state level. But, at the department level—where the real incentives or disincentives reside for faculty to work in the schools—important changes in promotion and tenure and in faculty workload policies are made.

At still other universities, you may find that adoption of a state-level policy, such as *Work in the Schools*, affects hiring practices of new faculty. Since expectations for new faculty are spelled out in original offer letters, inclusion of work in schools as part of accepted faculty workloads in a specific department can signal the beginning of change in institutional culture.

## CHANGES IN FACULTY PRACTICE

Gips (1998) wisely cautions that "Faculty concepts of their work are deeply situated in their academic mindsets and are not easily changed. Including K–12 work in the faculty roles and rewards system is not a fast-track change in academic governance and policy." Changes in policy and structures, while necessary, are insufficient.

Like most other people, university faculty do the work that is rewarded. Thus far, we have talked about how policy change—state-level and college-university-level—can be an important trigger of change in faculty behavior. What other incentives can you include in your STEM initiative to increase the real engagement of STEM faculty?

Four models are recommended. Each has been tested in practice: (1) involving STEM faculty in professional learning communities; (2) bringing STEM faculty together in state and regional Institute meetings; (3) bringing STEM faculty together in state and institution-led Academies for Learning; and (4) operating a competitive small-grants program. Regardless of the model used to increase engagement of STEM faculty, it should be stressed to them that increasing the number of students who are majors and successful graduates in science and mathematics is important to the future welfare of the nation.

### Professional Learning Communities

Chapter 6 includes multiple examples of professional learning communities in which higher education faculty could participate, both STEM and science and mathematics education faculty. If you are including K–16 professional learning communities in your STEM initiative, what incentives do you need to have to engage higher education faculty participation in them?

You could provide monetary incentives. Some faculty are responsive to receiving a stipend. Others—for whom time is the issue—may be more responsive to counting their participation in a K–16 learning communities as part of their workload.

### Institute on the Teaching and Learning of Science and Mathematics

Another useful strategy to use when trying to increase engagement of STEM faculty is to establish an Institute on the Teaching and Learning of Science and Mathematics (Institute). The Institute is a particular form of a learning community in which faculty can examine their own classroom practice, and can learn about, experiment with, and share various effective teaching approaches in science and mathematics that actively engage the learner, in ways on which others can build.

A statewide Institute typically is guided by a steering committee that sets the agenda based on input from the participants. A workable schedule is to hold one or two statewide two-day workshops annually. A useful initial focus is to invite those faculty members who teach introductory college courses in science and mathematics. These courses often are "gatekeepers" for students; that is, success in these courses is necessary for them to move forward to higher-level courses.

If you decide to include a statewide Institute in your STEM initiative, it is useful to organize the meetings around topics that build toward progressive understanding of what teaching practices need to change, why they need to change, and how STEM faculty may go about changing them. When faculty come to these Institute meetings, it is important to ask them their thoughts about the experience and then to use their feedback in planning future Institute meetings. In this way, you increase the likelihood of attendance of faculty members at future Institute meetings. Brief descriptions of Institute meetings in PRISM are given below.

If you include Institute meetings in your STEM initiative, it is important to choose speakers carefully. They must be credible national practitioners who can engage participants actively in the sessions. It is helpful if speakers model the behavior in their sessions that you are trying to promote in large-sized college classes in STEM fields. As your Institutes mature, it is also useful to provide time at them for your faculty to present and discuss their own effective practices in engaging students and increasing student understanding and enthusiasm for science and mathematics.

In addition to the statewide Institute, each college and university that is participating in your STEM initiative could set up a regional institute in order to stimulate ongoing initiatives and discussions in the time intervals between statewide meetings. For example, regional institutes could be used as reflective meetings as a follow up to the statewide Institute. Participants in the statewide Institute could share their experiences and learning with other colleagues, locally. You find it useful to include faculty from the sciences, mathematics, science education, mathematics education, and high school science and mathematics departments in both state-level and regional Institutes.

***PRISM Institute on the Teaching and Learning of Science and Mathematics.***    The first meeting in April 2004 featured plenary speakers who had served on National Research Council committees that produced *How People Learn* (Bransford et al. 1999) and *Knowing What Students Know* (Pellegrino et al. 2001). From this basic introduction to research findings that suggest that students at all levels build new knowledge and understanding on what they already know and believe, the second meeting in October 2004 was organized around common student misconceptions—how to identify them and strategies for addressing them in the classroom. In addition to plenary speakers, there were breakout workshops for biology, chemistry, and physics, and mathematics.

While we know that students have some misconceptions, we needed to know how to address their conceptions especially in large classes. The third meeting was held in February 2005 and its focus was on student assessment and use of scientific teaching through activities in large sections of introductory classes. The plenary talks were supplemented with two concurrent sessions where PRISM faculty presented some of their assessment initiatives. Attendance was limited to 100 participants at each statewide Institute, with twenty-five participants from each PRISM region.

### Academy for Learning

The Institutes just described are intended to strengthen faculty teaching in high school and in college introductory science and mathematics courses so as to enable a smoother student transition from high school to college in STEM fields. It is also important for your STEM initiative to include strategies that focus on enabling teachers, prepared in universities, to hit the ground running when they begin their teaching careers in the public schools.

A useful model is to help higher education faculty members in arts and sciences and in education to become familiar with a standards-based approach to teaching, as practiced in most school districts. One way to accomplish this is through including in your STEM initiative a statewide Academy for Learning through Performance Standards and Assessment (Academy).

One example is to organize your Academy so that it is designed and delivered to be outcomes-based using research-based principles and texts such as Huba and Freed (1999), Angelo and Cross (1993) and Wiggins and McTighe (2005). The purpose of the Academy is to help higher education faculty to focus on learning rather than on teaching. Through Academy meetings, faculty can learn strategies on how to redesign their courses to be learner-centered and to use assessment to improve learning.

Following the statewide academy meeting, individual colleges and universities that are participating can be encouraged to develop local academies and to expand participation to other science and mathematics faculty. An example of an institution Academy is given below.

*Georgia State University Academy for Learning.* A statewide Academy for Learning for over 100 higher education faculty from 23 University System of Georgia institutions was held in five three-day sessions from December 2005 to September 2006. An impetus for the Academy was the new Georgia Performance Standards (GPS) (see chapter 3). Most teams included faculty from colleges of arts and sciences and from colleges of education who were involved with teacher preparation. Since teachers are expected to deliver the new GPS through a standards-based approach, higher education faculty need to model a standards-based approach.

The Georgia State team distilled their key elements to create an assessment for learning environment that evolved into an institutional learning community involving seven STEM and five education faculty members. This learning community is organized and facilitated by the director of their center for teaching and learning and meets ten times per year.

This learning community is built on principles of assessment and has the following set of priorities for its members relative to classroom teaching. The assessment for learning team recognizes the importance of prior experience and learning, promotes the active engagement of the learner, engages students in big ideas, and provides specific, descriptive rapid feedback about learning.

As a result of this cross-college learning community, five chemistry faculty who teach an introductory course have formed a lesson study group (Cerbin and Kopp 2008) to improve learning of thermo-chemistry. They are being convened by one of the STEM faculty who is a regular member of the learning community. In addition, each semester, the Academy has organized an all-day workshop for instructors of introductory science and mathematics courses. The focus has been on increasing student engagement and learning.

## Small Grants Program

Perhaps the most important way of engaging higher education faculty in your K–16 STEM initiative and in invigorating introductory college courses in science and mathematics is through a small grants program. If you include this model in your STEM initiative, you find it useful to make your small grants competitive and to support a range of faculty activities. For example, you could make small grants available for higher education faculty to (1) modify introductory STEM college courses to include more inquiry and active learning, (2) develop new assessment strategies to improve student learning, and (3) investigate some aspect of science or mathematics teaching in K–12 schools such as selecting a concept in mathematics or science that is particularly challenging to teach because the concept has common misconceptions or is abstract in nature.

The small grants are typically in the range from $2,000 to $30,000 with an average of about $8,000. Awarded funds could be used, for example, for faculty salaries, graduate assistant stipends, professional travel, and materials needed for the project. In addition to providing resources, small grants represent peer recognition of a faculty member's efforts to improve K–16 STEM education. Examples of the power of the small grants program are given below.

In order to encourage participants to consider effective practices in describing their work, a structured abstract is a useful format to expect faculty to use for reporting findings from small grant projects. The structured abstract is an innovative and informative tool to help disseminate education studies and research findings in a format that is clearer than the traditional abstract. The structured abstract consists of a nine-component template that may help bridge the worlds of education research and practice (Mosteller et al. 2004).

**PRISM Small Grants Program.**   The Northeast (NE) Georgia region initiated small grants in summer 2004 to provide funding to higher education faculty for innovative projects related to improving instruction and student learning in science and mathematics at the undergraduate level. Twenty proposals were funded in this initial round. The request for proposals was broad in order to capture wide-spread interest. The program was designed to (1) promote participation in the state PRISM Institute for Teaching and Learning of Science and Mathematics and support the work throughout the year; and (2) focus efforts to stimulate change in undergraduate courses.

The other regions followed the NE Georgia region's lead and developed their own small grants programs, in all cases extending the scope of the proposals to include improving instruction and student learning in K–12 schools. In all four regions, there had to be at least one higher education faculty member associated with a small grants project.

In the initial round of regional small grant proposals, forty-three science and mathematics faculty were funded. Of these faculty, it was the first time that thirty-four of them had been involved in implementing new teaching strategies or in working with K–12 teachers. Many of the projects yielded results that were reported in peer-reviewed publications and at professional conferences. As of November 2007, over fifteen articles stimulated by small grants have been accepted for publication in peer-reviewed journals.

Other practices that you can consider to engage STEM faculty include (1) informal meetings between members of your project leadership team and individuals or small groups of faculty to discuss the small grants project and the opportunities for involvement, (2) a monthly faculty roundtable forum that focuses on topics related to the scholarship of teaching and learning, (3) the yearly regional institutes at which faculty describe the results of their small grants projects and learn about innovative approaches to the delivery and assessment of instruction. The practices for engaging faculty that have been discussed in this section provide a menu of options for consideration when designing your systemic K–16 STEM initiative.

## INDICATORS OF SUCCESS

As you launch strategies to increase and sustain the engagement of higher education faculty in your STEM initiative, it is important at the outset to determine your indicators of success. For example, in PRISM, several indicators are used to assess success of engaging higher education faculty in the activities of the project. The adoption of the statewide *Work in the Schools* policy is a major achievement that provides a clear signal to faculty in Georgia that working on K–16 education reform is valued and should be appropriately rewarded. Regional practices such as professional learning communities and small grants programs have attracted substantial numbers of previously uninvolved faculty into the K–16 STEM education tent. Faculty interest in the scholarship of teaching and learning has grown as evidenced by the surge in scholarly productivity in this area.

A very tangible measure of the impact of PRISM is the provision of funding from the Board of Regents of the University System of Georgia through its new STEM Initiative to replicate the K–16 professional learning communities and small grants programs on a statewide level. All University System of Georgia institutions that offer the associate or baccalaureate degree with approved majors in STEM fields or middle grades and high school teacher preparation programs in science and mathematics are eligible to participate.

The success of PRISM in increasing higher education faculty involvement in K–16 STEM education reform in Georgia has resulted from changes in system and institutional policies (top-down change) and college and departmental practices (bottom-up change). This participation by multiple levels of stakeholders (Appendix 7.1) is necessary to effect a meaningful change in the culture of higher education. Will faculty involvement in K–16 work be sustained beyond the life of PRISM? While it is still too early to answer this important question, the initial signs are promising (see chapter 9).

## RECOMMENDED ACTION ITEMS

In summary, the following action items are recommended for consideration by those designing a faculty reward structure for their institution or state system.

- When assembling the committee that leads this strategy, enlist individuals with the authority and expertise to move your agenda forward.
- During the design stage, seek input from a broad spectrum of stakeholders at various levels in your institution or from different institutions in your state system.
- Be flexible in designing your reward system; recognize that one size does not fit all even within a single institution.
- Build upon existing initiatives at the institutional, state, and national levels; join forces with those who can help you achieve your goals.
- Adopt strategies that result in top-down and bottom-up changes in the culture of your institution or state system.
- Employ strategies such as involving faculty in professional learning communities; bringing faculty together in statewide and local Institute meetings; bringing faculty together in state and institution's Academy for Learning; and operating a competitive small grants program.

## NOTE

1. Charles Kutal is a regional co-principal investigator in the Partnership for Reform In Science and Mathematics (PRISM), a systemic K–16 STEM initiative in Georgia. He is a professor of chemistry and Associate Dean of the College of Arts and Sciences at the University of Georgia. Fred Rich is a regional co-principal investigator in PRISM. He is a professor of geology at Georgia Southern University. He is a palynologist and paleoecologist by training, but has had a long interest in earth science education for teachers. He is currently affiliated with the St. Catherines Island (GA) Sea Turtle Conservation Program. Sabrina A. Hessinger is a regional co-principal investigator in PRISM. She is an associate professor of mathematics and Special Assistant to the Dean of the College of Science and Technology in charge of the STEM Initiative at Armstrong Atlantic State University in Savannah. H. Richard Miller is a regional co-principal investigator in PRISM. He is an astrophysicist and chair of the Department of Physics and Astronomy at Georgia State University in Atlanta.

# 8

# EVALUATING A COMPREHENSIVE SYSTEMIC INITIATIVE TO IMPROVE K–16 SCIENCE AND MATHEMATICS TEACHING AND LEARNING

Judith A. Monsaas and Mary Jo McGee-Brown[1]

## INTRODUCTION

Evaluation is a critical component in the development and implementation of any reform. Program evaluation has been in use for a long time, and there are methodologies for evaluating programs clearly articulated in program evaluation texts (e.g., Rossi et al. 2003; Worthen et al. 2003) and in *The Program Evaluation Standards* (Sanders 1994). The unique challenge, described in this chapter, is how to evaluate a complex multi-site, multi-objective, systemic reform initiative, specifically in science, technology, engineering, and mathematics (STEM) fields.

There are challenges that emerge as an evaluation team designs and implements an evaluation plan for a systemic STEM reform initiative. Some challenges that are addressed in this chapter include:

- The evaluation of partnerships. Program evaluation commonly focuses on program implementation and outcomes. Increasingly, a goal of systemic reform projects has been the development of collaborative and effective partnerships. Partnership evaluation must examine roles and inputs of each partner, benefits to each partner, and the value-added for a partnership approach rather than each unit working alone to enhance school-college (K–16) student learning. The evaluation design must address different facets of the partnerships.

- Evaluation of multi-level, multi-institution collaborations. Systemic reform initiatives, by definition, include multiple levels of participants from across diverse institutions. A particular challenge in the design and implementation of a project evaluation plan is to determine strategies to ensure evaluation of effectiveness within and across K–16 levels, schools and colleges of different sizes and with different missions, and regional and state levels. A multi-level, multi-method, but integrated design is required to meet this challenge.
- The evaluation of implementation. While program implementation has long been an important focus for evaluation, the task may prove to be particularly complex and elusive for a systemic reform project with varied activities across sites and institutions. In many cases, there may be different experiences and outcomes for individual participants as customized professional learning is designed and delivered to meet targeted student needs in multiple sites.
- The evaluation of policy change. On the surface, this would appear easy to evaluate—was the new policy implemented? Yes or No. However, to understand the success of a new policy, evaluators must focus on how policy is developed, the role of partnerships in its development and implementation, and how policy is implemented across sites. Whether and how culture is changed to facilitate policy implementation is critical to the evaluation. Most everyone is aware of policies that are only "on the books" and are ignored because there has been no substantive culture change.
- The interrelationship of all project components. Understanding the interrelationship among project components must be a priority at the design and early implementation phases. Some components initially may need to be evaluated independently, yet as the project progresses and components merge in various ways, the evaluation must evolve and reflect such change to be most effective. Evaluators must be keenly aware of the interaction effects of various project strategies throughout implementation. They must also be aware of the interaction effects of partnerships.

Clearly, one evaluator's challenge is another evaluator's opportunity. This chapter is a "how to" for designing and conducting complex, multi-level, systemic evaluations, using examples from the Partnership for Reform In Science and Mathematics (PRISM) project. PRISM is a National Science Foundation (NSF) comprehensive project designed to improve teaching and learning in science and mathematics at the K–12 and college levels in four very different regions across the state. PRISM has multiple objectives and strategies adding to the complexity. Ideas presented in this chapter reflect lessons learned in the PRISM evaluation.

## HOW TO EVALUATE A LARGE-SCALE MULTI-SITE STEM INITIATIVE

It is critical that evaluators work closely with the project leaders to ensure that all partners are working toward the same goals. Evaluators must be brought in during all phases of planning for a number of reasons:

- Evaluators can make sure project goals and objectives are measurable;
- Baseline data must be gathered before the project is implemented or in the early stages of the project to enable evidence of change over time and of program effectiveness;
- When evaluators work closely with the project leaders in developing plans and instruments, evaluators are viewed as part of the team, and the buy-in of stakeholders is strengthened; and
- Logic models and other representational forms for showing connections that evaluators have in their toolkits can help the project leaders identify relationships among partners, strategies, goals, etc. This can help provide coherence to the overall initiative when writing about or explaining the project to other team members and interested parties.

Suggested steps for evaluating a complex STEM initiative are as follows—a recommendation is that evaluators not skip any of the steps listed:

Step 1: Identify scope of the evaluation. Develop logic models and evaluation plans.

Step 2: Identify the evaluation design and the nature of the data to be gathered.

Step 3: Assemble a complementary evaluation team to meet the needs of the project.

Step 4: Develop evaluation plans, timelines, etc. Develop and identify instruments.

Step 5: Conduct evaluation and provide ongoing feedback to the project leadership.

Step 6. Write annual summative evaluation reports to stakeholders and funders.

***Step 1: Identify the Scope of the Evaluation.***    Stakeholders find the evaluation to be more valuable and use the findings if they are involved in all stages of the planning. Conceptual or logic models can be helpful in identifying the relationships among the various strategies and activities and the desired outcomes of your STEM project. In addition, a "living logic model" can help project leaders and evaluators see the relationships among various components of the project and evaluation; it can help participants understand how data-gathering is tied to project goals and outcomes.

An example of an evaluation logic model can be found in Figure 8.1. It shows how the various components of PRISM and data-gathering are related. Logic models are best used as "living" documents in that they typically go through several iterations. The logic model shown here is currently used in a simplified version to describe the relationships among PRISM inputs and strategies and outcomes (see chapter 1).

Logic models can take numerous forms. A useful resource to use when developing the logic model for your STEM initiative is that used by the National Science Foundation (Frechtling 2002). A simple logic model is recommended that has at least four categories: inputs, activities, short-term outcomes, and long-term outcomes. Keep in mind, though, that the logic model developed at the beginning of your STEM initiative changes over time, as data are gathered by your evaluation team and used to give feedback to your STEM leadership team about which activities have been most successful and what forms of implementation have worked and not worked.

*Inputs and resources.* Inputs include the various partners and the resources they bring to the project. One of the major resources to consider is any form of grant funding. It is very helpful to identify all partners early in the process to make sure all important stakeholders have input in planning. Additional partners and resources are typically added as the project progresses, and some may be dropped or discontinued.

*Activities.* In many evaluations, the project activities are fairly simple and straightforward, such as implementing professional development for high school teachers who teach Algebra. The logic model in Figure 8.1 gives a realistic sampling of the activities that are likely to be included in your systemic STEM initiative. The role of the evaluators is to document the implementation of activities and provide feedback to the project leaders on the effectiveness of the various activities, whether your STEM initiative has one focus or many.

*Short-term outcomes.* Short-term outcomes have a variety of forms depending on the project. They could include simple outcomes like "200 new middle grades mathematics teachers are prepared" or more complex

# PRISM Evaluation Logic Model

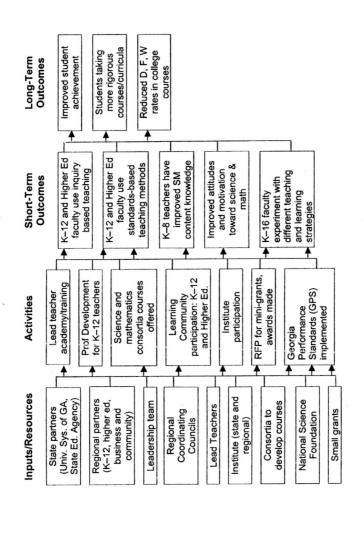

| Inputs/Resources | Activities | Short-Term Outcomes | Long-Term Outcomes |
|---|---|---|---|
| State partners (Univ. Sys. of GA, State Ed. Agency) | Lead teacher academy/training | K–12 and Higher Ed faculty use inquiry based teaching | Improved student achievement |
| Regional partners (K–12, higher ed, business and community) | Prof Development for K–12 teachers | K–12 and Higher Ed faculty use standards-based teaching methods | Students taking more rigorous courses/curricula |
| Leadership team | Science and mathematics consortia courses offered | K–8 teachers have improved SM content knowledge | Reduced D, F, W rates in college courses |
| Regional Coordinating Councils | Learning Community participation: K–12 and Higher Ed. | Improved attitudes and motivation toward science & math | |
| Lead Teachers | Institute participation | K–16 faculty experiment with different teaching and learning strategies | |
| Institute (state and regional) | RFP for mini-grants, awards made | | |
| Consortia to develop courses | Georgia Performance Standards (GPS) implemented | | |
| National Science Foundation | | | |
| Small grants | | | |

Formative Evaluation    Summative Evaluation

**Figure 8.1.  PRISM evaluation logic model**

outcomes, such as "K–16 faculty members use more effective teaching and learning strategies." For PRISM, teacher change was viewed as the major short-term outcome. The PRISM leaders and evaluators wanted to know if K–16 faculty were implementing what they had learned in the professional development in their own classrooms. Specifically, were teachers using more inquiry? Were they using standards-based teaching and learning? Did stronger science and mathematics content knowledge improve their delivery of instruction?

*Long-term outcomes.* Long-term outcomes are the changes that might not be expected to emerge until some time after the project experiences have been completed. The bottom line typically is: Did student achievement improve? While an immediate impact on student achievement in science and mathematics cannot be expected to happen, with a five-year project the expectation should be that some improvement in student learning in science and mathematics should be observed at the K–12 and college levels by the end of the five years.

**Step 2: Identify the Evaluation Design and the Nature of the Data to Be Gathered.**    The evaluation design and the nature of the data gathered are dependent upon the project goals and objectives. The logic model can help identify the design as well. Again, it is important that evaluators work closely with project leaders to ensure that the design is feasible and provides the types of information needed by the project leaders and funders.

Evaluation designs may include quantitative or qualitative assessment, but most include a combination of the two, called mixed-method designs. Using qualitative and quantitative methods creates multiple lenses that contribute to meaningful tracking and exploration of program implementation and validation of important program outcomes. Johnson and Onwuegbuzie (2004) cite several strengths of using a mixed-method design. Such designs can (1) combine the strengths of both quantitative and qualitative designs to create a more comprehensive design, (2) answer a broader range of research and evaluation questions, (3) provide stronger evidence for conclusions through convergence and corroboration of findings, (4) provide insights that might be missed when a single method is used, and (5) increase the generalizability of the findings.

The complex nature of evaluations of systemic STEM initiatives makes it clear that a mixed-methods design is needed. Early in a project, a team of evaluators needs to be identified that has the varied types of expertise needed to evaluate a project with multiple types of implementation and outcomes.

The quantitative methods that are strongly encouraged by the National Science Foundation (NSF) include Randomized Field Trials. While these designs can be used to make a strong case for causation, they are frequently impractical and not feasible. When randomized designs are not possible, a strong quasi-experimental design provides evidence for causal relationships (Shadish et al. 2002). In a large-scale project, often the implementation of activities does not begin in all participating school districts and colleges at the same time. Instead participation is more likely phased in. This allows your evaluators to use those that are not yet participating as comparison schools and colleges for those that are participating. If a school is implementing programs in specific classrooms, a district in specific schools, or districts within a state, a matched set of nonparticipating classrooms, schools, etc., can be compared to obtain causal inferences. And as Chatterji (2004) points out, extended-term, mixed-method designs can strengthen those causal conclusions.

It is recommended that evaluators explore the possibility of random assignment of classes (or schools or districts) to treatments. If not possible, they should identify non-participating classes to serve as controls. It is important that the classes, schools, and districts be carefully matched. Some variables suggested for matching are: prior student achievement, percent minority, a measure of socio-economic status (typically percent on free and reduced-price lunch), and district size. If you have access to school-level achievement test scores in your state, school districts and schools can be matched using propensity scores (Rosenbaum and Rubin 1983; Hahs-Vaughn and Onwuegbuzie 2006), using district size, percent minority, and percent on free and reduced-price lunch to obtain comparable schools for numerous analyses. Linear regression would be a reasonable substitute for propensity score analysis to identify matching schools.

Qualitative evaluation is an essential component for a systemic STEM initiative. It is an assumption for all systemic projects that no project component is implemented equally across individuals, institutions, sites, or time. Thus, qualitative case studies are critical for understanding what is implemented, how, and how effectively within diverse project contexts over time. Ideally, there is a qualitative evaluator for every one or two sites or regions within a project, and at least one examining holistically the large-scale implementation. This triangulation of evaluators allows for more in-depth collection of evaluation data. Qualitative evaluators use purposeful sampling to collect data from sources and situations that provide data to address specific evaluation questions.

Qualitative data-collection methods provide different types of data necessary for understanding the effectiveness of the whole project implementation.

Selection of appropriate methods is critical (Patton 2002). Participant observation enables the evaluator to meet and observe participants in specific contexts as they implement project strategies and determine the nature and effectiveness of partnerships in action. While interviews (individual and focus groups) enable the evaluator to understand in depth different individuals' project experiences and perspectives, complementing them with open-ended questionnaires provides additional broader understanding through comparative data from larger groups of participants. Document analysis provides the evaluator with implementation and policy data from across groups and institutions.

**Step 3: Assemble a Complementary Evaluation Team to Meet the Needs of the Project.**    Evaluation team building is a seminal part of any systemic evaluation. As the project leaders and evaluation consultants determine the types of expertise necessary for a well-rounded team of evaluators to cover all project components and address each measurable project goal, they should use a general set of guiding questions to identify necessary areas of evaluation expertise. General guiding questions for collaborative decision-making might include, but not be limited to, the following. Does any project goal require an evaluator with:

- Knowledge of culture and social theory, expertise in qualitative research and evaluation design, and experience in applying multiple qualitative data analysis strategies?
- Expertise and experience in constructing surveys and other types of data-collection instruments?
- Expertise and experience in designing and implementing case study methods to determine impact on different project sites?
- Knowledge of various quantitative research and evaluation designs for making causal inferences?
- Advanced statistical expertise?
- Access to various student and faculty, K–12 and higher education, district or state level databases including K–12 standardized assessment?

When the project leaders have clearly defined project goals and expectations and determined all areas of evaluator expertise necessary to address each goal, the process of identifying evaluators with those strengths can begin. With a multi-site, multi-year, multi-strategy project, using multiple lenses to evaluate project effectiveness is essential.

In addition the evaluators may be called upon by project leaders to help participants use data for planning and improvement, assist with action research, and provide both qualitative (e.g., survey and interview) and quantitative (e.g., statistical analyses) assistance. If there is a publication expectation, the evaluators may be expected to assist project leaders in developing articles and presentations and preparing publications themselves.

Many higher education faculty, including mathematicians and scientists, may be unfamiliar with social science theory, philosophy, and research strategies but want to conduct contextualized classroom research. Their research adds to important project impact insights but guidance may be required. The skills needed by the combined members of the evaluation team are heavily influenced by an expectation to provide such research help.

A collaborative evaluation team model—including multiple external evaluators, multiple internal evaluators, and project site-based evaluators—is found to be very effective. External evaluators in this model have no professional connection to any project partner schools or colleges. Internal evaluators are in professional research and evaluation positions within partner institutions, and thus, have access to databases important to the project evaluation. Internal project site-based evaluators hold professional positions in core partner institutions of higher education and can assist in data-gathering in the various project locations.

Since external evaluators frequently do not have direct access to state K–12 student performance and teacher demographic databases or partner higher education databases, it is critical to identify internal evaluation team members who do have access to these data and who can write programs to pull essential data from the broad databases that inform evaluation questions and benchmarks.

The state internal and external evaluators must meet regularly to discuss methodology, evaluation issues, and findings across regions, and to ensure evaluators working on various aspects of the evaluation are gathering comparable information. Establishing monthly evaluation team meetings, with regular e-mail contact, is recommended. If evaluators are spread out across the state, this is a reasonable frequency to balance the amount of time spent traveling and the need for coordination across the project. A multi-state project should consider using other types of video or electronic means for some of these meetings and discussions.

It is not possible to evaluate everything in a complex project, and decisions must be made concerning what to evaluate. To help with this, it is important that evaluators meet regularly with project leaders. In addition, project leaders can be invited to attend evaluation team meetings and one or two evaluators can attend program planning and implementation meetings.

In short, recommendations are (a) identify a team of evaluators who have the varied skill sets needed by the project, (b) meet regularly as a team to make sure data that need to be comparable are comparable, and (c) coordinate the variation based on unique implementation of project goals. It is also important that a senior project leader meet regularly with the evaluators and evaluation representatives meet with the project leadership.

**Step 4: Develop Evaluation Plans, Timelines, etc. Develop and Identify Instruments.**    A mixed-method quantitative-qualitative evaluation design is described here because of the complexity of a systemic STEM initiative and because of the need to understand the process of implementing change in diverse regions of a state. One assumption made here is that all of the strategies included in your system STEM initiative focus on improving teaching and learning. A second assumption is that many of your strategies involve providing various activities for K–16 faculty members to improve content and pedagogy. A third assumption is that these professional activities for faculty (workshops, content courses, professional learning communities, and small grants awarded to teachers and faculty to try new teaching strategies and conduct action research on their effectiveness) include an effort to improve teaching and learning in the classroom at both K–12 and higher education.

Based on the previous assumptions, an example of evaluation questions and data-gathering procedures are in Table 8.1. The categories in this table are adapted from Guskey's (2000) book on *Evaluating Professional Development*. Guskey argues that many evaluations of professional development focus on how the participants viewed the professional development and do not move to the next levels of use of the knowledge and skills and impact on student learning.

Data sources in a systemic project evaluation should include K–12 and higher education faculty and administrators, leadership teams and project partners across levels (institutions, districts, regions, state), and parent and community participants. Data-collection methods appropriate to each evaluation question should be selected from among existing databases, documents, observations, surveys, questionnaires, interviews (individual and focus groups), participant sign-in sheets, and partner self-evaluation rubrics. Some of the types of data that are important to provide a comprehensive evaluation include:

*Participant information.* This is often a challenge to an evaluation team but is critical to the success of the evaluation because it is necessary to know who participated in what to link faculty participation to the various outcome variables. A strong recommendation is to set up a robust database system or, preferably, a data mart where the data from several sources can be con-

**Table 8.1. Evaluation of PRISM Professional Learning Questions and Procedures**

| Evaluation Question | Data-Gathering Procedure |
|---|---|
| Who participated in PRISM activities? | PRISM Participant Information Form |
| To what extent? | Participant rosters |
| What was the nature of the professional learning? | Agendas, syllabi, reading lists<br>Qualitative data including observation<br>Participant rating forms |
| How effective was the professional learning activity? | Surveys<br>Observation |
| Did the participants acquire the intended knowledge and skills? | Inventory of Teaching and Learning (ITAL)<br>Content assessments<br>Open-ended questionnaires/surveys<br>Qualitative data |
| Did the participants use the acquired knowledge and skills in the classroom? | ITAL<br>Reformed Teacher Observation Protocol (RTOP)<br>Open-ended questionnaires/surveys<br>Qualitative data |
| Did student achievement improve? | Georgia Criterion Referenced Competency Tests (CRCTs)<br>High School Graduation Tests (GHSGT)<br>High school course-taking patterns.<br>D, W, F rates in college courses<br>College course progression |

nected to answer the evaluation questions with respect to different activities. As an example, one goal of the PRISM evaluation has been to determine what is effective for whom under what conditions. Without careful tracking of who participates in what, this question is impossible to answer.

*Documents.* To understand the nature of each project strategy, it is important to know what took place during training and classroom implementation. Agendas, syllabi, reading lists, meeting reports, instructional and assessment documents, new state policies (and revised institution and department policies to reflect new state policy) are all important data for putting together the pieces of the puzzle.

*Participant rating forms.* Evaluation surveys are typically administered to determine how effective the project activities were for the participants. In addition to asking the typical customer service types of questions, it is important to ask participants to reflect on what they learned and how they would use what they learned when they returned to their classroom, school, or institution.

*Information on practice.* In addition to obtaining information on participants' perceptions and plans, it is important for evaluators to determine if the participants use what they have learned when they return to the class-room. The two primary methods for obtaining these data are self-report and observation. Studies examining the accuracy of teachers' self-reports present mixed results (Ross et al. 2003), although some of these results are attributed to weak research designs. You may find, for example, that teachers claim greater use of effective teaching and learning strategies than is observed in their classrooms. One article reported that teacher self-reports reflect not only their behaviors but also their espoused ideals (Wubbels et al. 1992). For this reason, if resources permit, evaluators should include both self-report and observational data-gathering in their plans.

As an example, the *Inventory of Teaching and Learning (ITAL)* is an instrument developed by members of the PRISM evaluation team. It is a fifty-two-item questionnaire and is a self-report instrument on teachers' emphasis on standards-based, inquiry-based, and traditional teaching and learning practices. For detailed information on the instrument and its development, please see Ellett and Monsaas (2007).

When using a self-report instrument such as the *ITAL*, it can be matched with an observational instrument like the *Reformed Teacher Observation Protocol (RTOP)* to obtain direct information on teachers' and university facultys' use of inquiry in the classroom. Classroom observations can be used to determine if teachers and faculty are implementing inquiry-based teaching and learning in their classrooms. The *Reformed Teaching Observation Protocol* (Sawada et al. 2000) was developed at Arizona State University by the Arizona Collaborative for Excellence in the Preparation of Teachers. It was designed as an observation framework to guide data collection using twenty-five indicators of reformed teaching and learning environments in science and mathematics classrooms.

If you decide to use a direct observational instrument, like the *RTOP*, you may find it difficult to implement if your STEM initiative includes multiple forms of professional development and multiple outcomes for different participants. In a large-scale project, the cost of sampling a large number of K–16 faculty may also be prohibitive. If your evaluation budget is limited, allowing you only to complete a small number of observations at each grade level (elementary, middle, high school, and college) in both science and mathematics, it may make it difficult to draw any generalizations from the data.

You may also find that the participants in your STEM initiative are experiencing data-collection overload, making use of a direct observational instrument (that is more intrusive and labor intensive) less desirable. It still is important to gather direct observational data where the number of professional learning activities is more focused or where a large budget can make sure that an adequate sample can be obtained, and ideally, teachers can be paid a minimal stipend for agreeing to be observed.

*Open-ended questionnaires.* Open-ended questionnaires and open-ended questions on surveys provide essential in-depth and descriptive information about individual participants' experiences across project activities. This format allows acquisition of data from large numbers of participants, and when the same instrument is used across sites and regions, comparative analysis can reveal differences or similarities in implementation and impact.

*Interviews.* Individual and focus group interviews are particularly useful if you want to discover more in-depth understandings about an individual's contextualized experiences. The interviewer can follow up on issues raised by the interviewee. Interviews are more labor intensive than open-ended questionnaires, thus, the sample is necessarily smaller using this method. However, analysis of information gathered during interviews can result in categories that can provide direction for developing open-ended questionnaires that more closely reflect participants' experiences. This can result in better quality questionnaire data.

*Student assessments.* Obtaining student achievement data, while necessary, is often a challenge in many evaluations. This is especially true since it is frequently difficult to link student achievement to changes implemented by project participants (e.g., K–16 faculty). The ideal situation is to have individual student-level assessment data that is linked to teacher participation data within a school or university course. Frequently, data at this level are not available.

For example, if school-level scores on state accountability assessments are available to the evaluators of your STEM initiative, but individual student-level data are not provided through the state, it is not possible to link the data to individual teachers who each participated in different project activities. In this situation, student performance data are not as useful as they would be if they could be linked to the teachers who actually participate in the specific activities included in your STEM initiative.

A common occurrence in states that may impact the use of student performance data is a revision of the state curriculum that requires subsequent revisions of the state assessments. Another situation is that test standards (cut scores) are occasionally changed making pass rates from year to year not comparable. When these situations occur, with implementation of each new set of performance standards (e.g., third grade mathematics), there is a new assessment. These new assessments that reflect a different curriculum likely have new test items, have new cut scores, and are on a different scale, preclude comparisons with previous years' test performance.

If you find yourself in these kinds of situations, you can compare test data from participating and nonparticipating school districts using matched propensity score analysis on the basis of school district size, percent of students on free and reduced-price lunches, and percent minority. These districts and schools can be compared to determine the effect of your STEM initiative on student achievement levels. Additional analyses comparing schools with different activities (e.g., learning communities, professional development, and small grants) can be conducted. Participating schools can be rated by "levels of intervention" and compared to non-participating schools to determine what level of implementation needs to be provided to improve student achievement.

In addition to identifying the evaluation questions and data-gathering procedures, very specific evaluation work plans need to be developed for each of the strategies in your STEM initiative including columns in the work plan for evaluation questions, data sources, samples, participants, responsible parties, and due dates.

**Step 5: Conduct Evaluation and Provide Ongoing Feedback to the Project Leadership.**   On an ongoing basis, data must be gathered using the evaluation plan and regular feedback needs to be provided to all stakeholders. Annual reports and case studies are particularly helpful to provide ongoing formative feedback on activities to project leaders. If your STEM initiative includes both state-level leaders and regional and local leaders, it is also important for regional and local feedback to be provided to regional and local leaders on an ongoing basis. Interim case studies can be provided to regional, local, and state leaders. By spacing out the extensive qualitative reporting into more frequent mini-case studies, the evaluators can prepare occasional reports on special topics such as partnerships, Lead Teachers, and sustainability, in addition to reporting on the overall effectiveness of project strategies and activities.

In short, there are three levels of feedback that typically prove useful to the regional and local and state leaders in large-scale STEM projects: ongoing feedback from surveys and interviews provided as the data are analyzed; formative evaluation reports prepared during the year to give a broad picture of what is working and not working; and summative reports that include annual reports prepared to funders. Note that in a multi-year project, these annual summative reports are also formative.

**Step 6: Write Annual Summative Evaluation Reports to Stakeholders and Funders.**   Annual reports are usually required by funders and stakeholders, and these evaluation reports are traditionally comprehensive and lengthy. It is important for evaluators to develop formats for distilling their findings from the evaluation for readers who are not interested in reading a 100-plus-page evaluation report. An executive summary, with no more than a page allotted for each strategy and topic, is an effective reporting method for those readers interested in just the bottom line. Then the more extensive reports, with methods and back-up data, can be made available for the readers who want more information.

## OTHER TOPICS TO CONSIDER IN EVALUATING SYSTEMIC STEM INITIATIVES

*Participants' generation and use of data.* Partnerships in systemic STEM initiatives include higher education faculty from STEM colleges and colleges of education as well as K–12 science and mathematics teachers. Many contextualized questions about effectiveness of classroom implementation of project strategies arise for individual instructors. Many want to conduct their own research to determine effectiveness of best practices they are implementing. However, most do not have a background in social science research. Evaluator team members with expertise in action research methods can facilitate workshops for project participants on design, data-collection methods, and data analysis strategies appropriate for classroom-level research.

K–16 faculty are increasingly making data-based decisions. In addition to K–12 teachers using student standardized test data to generate school improvement plans and university faculty using data to try to increase student success in STEM introductory courses, all educators in a systemic STEM initiative should consider using formative and summative evaluation data to guide decision-making about best practices in instruction and assessment. Thus, it is important for evaluation teams to make raw data available to educators at all levels of a project as well as to share evaluation reports with them.

*Building Evaluation Capacity.* Evaluation Capacity-Building (ECB), an important topic in the evaluation community, is tied to the discussion above related to participant data use. According to King (2007),

> the goal of ECB is to strengthen and sustain effective program evaluation practices through a number of activities: (1) increasing an organization's capacity to design, implement, and manage effective evaluation projects; (2) accessing, building, and using evaluative knowledge and skills; (3) cultivating a spirit of continuous organizational learning, improvement and accountability; and (4) creating awareness and support for evaluation as a performance improvement strategy. (45–46)

Evaluators need to be aware that in addition to learning from their evaluation findings, project leaders and participants learn about the evaluation process. Some evaluators have referred to this as ECB learning and teaching strategies (Preskill 2008). The evaluation team should be very purposeful in working with the project leaders and stakeholders to be sure they use the evaluation results and develop the skills needed to conduct their own mini-evaluations of various projects. The skills provided, both formally and informally, by the evaluators can be used by the project leaders to conduct their own research and evaluation. Should this occur in your STEM initiative, it is important for it to be coordinated with and supplemented by your evaluation team. The evaluators should share evidence, where ethics permit, for project leaders who wish to publish results for a particular strategy and perhaps present and publish with project leaders.

Because it is important in systemic STEM initiatives to base decisions on evidence, the evaluation team must provide the data and evaluation reports to the project leaders so programmatic decisions can be based on evidence. The evaluators can also support project participants who are collecting evidence on the effectiveness of their own classroom practices.

Preskill (2008, 132), in the American Evaluation Association presidential address, identified eight processes and activities to ensure that ECB efforts are successful:

- Have clear goals and objectives;
- Reflect adult learning principles and recognize that learning is experiential as well as cognitive;
- Foster transfer of learning back to the job;
- Include dialog, reflection, and feedback;
- Consider different learning styles;
- Take into account the cultural context and be culturally responsive;
- Employ facilitators who are trusted, respected, and humble; and
- Provide adequate time for learning.

ECB, when considered in planning and implementing an evaluation, can provide an effective form of professional learning for teachers, faculty, administrators, and project leaders.

## STEPS IN DESIGNING AND IMPLEMENTING EFFECTIVE EVALUATION

This chapter concludes with the following guidelines with action steps for building a successful evaluation plan for your systemic STEM initiative.

The purposeful building of an evaluation team is essential to the success of evaluation of a multi-level, multi-site, multi-year STEM initiative. It is important for evaluators to:

- Meet with project leaders in initial planning sessions;
- Help project leaders identify measurable goals and timelines for all strategies;
- Identify areas of evaluation expertise necessary to evaluate all goals;
- Create a team of evaluators with necessary qualitative or quantitative expertise to cover all project sites and data collection for all strategies;
- Have monthly evaluation team meetings and invite the project director to attend; and
- Function in a truly collaborative fashion.

Another critical phase in the planning for a systemic evaluation is to secure the appropriate authorization for data collection in all partner institutions including:

- Identify the Internal Research Board (IRB) requirements at all partner schools and colleges;
- Submit all evaluation instruments to appropriate IRB personnel for approval;
- Ensure all evaluators are current in IRB protocol; and
- Inform key university and school district administrators that IRB regulations are being followed to protect all project participants.

Finally, develop a plan for sharing the evaluation design and findings with partners throughout the project.

- Share the evaluation plan and instruments with state and regional leaders early in the project;
- Share formative and yearly evaluation reports with regional and state leaders;
- Provide a formal mechanism for leaders to respond to evaluation reports;
- Share raw data (except when promised confidentiality would be compromised) with partners who need them for local decision-making, professional presentations or publications; and
- Share evaluation findings with the national STEM community through professional presentations, articles, and books.

It is essential to develop a complete evaluation plan to examine in a holistic manner all that a systemic STEM initiative implements. However, staying flexible enough to change the plan or add different data-collection strategies or instruments as the project evolves over multiple years is key to the success of the evaluation team. The evaluation team must be a true partnership, with qualitative and quantitative evaluators continually identifying ways their strategies and resulting data support the other in broadening and giving more depth of understanding about effectiveness of reform strategies in STEM education.

## NOTE

1. Judith A. Monsaas is the lead evaluator of the Partnership for Reform In Science and Mathematics (PRISM), a systemic K–16 STEM initiative in Georgia. She is a professor of education specializing in evaluation, assessment, statistics, and research and is the executive director for P–16 Evaluation and Assessment for the University System of Georgia. Mary Jo McGee-Brown is the lead external qualitative evaluator of PRISM. She is the president of Qualitative Research & Evaluation for Action, Inc., and formerly taught Qualitative Research and Data Analysis at the University of Georgia.

# BRINGING A K–16 STEM INITIATIVE TO SCALE

*Ronald J. Henry[1]*

## INTRODUCTION

**M**ost states have long histories of trying various educational reform initiatives designed to improve student learning and achievement. Some have taken root in local practices in schools and colleges. But, more often than not, especially when special funding is brought in to launch the initiative, it dies when funding ends.

In *The Seven Habits of Highly Effective People*, Covey (1989) states "Begin with the end in mind." As you plan a systemic K–16 STEM initiative in your state, it is important to attend to issues of sustainability and bringing your initiative to scale from the very beginning of your planning. Coburn (2003) suggests that to bring a reform initiative to scale, four interrelated dimensions need to be addressed: depth, sustainability, spread, and shift in ownership. One important component of sustainability is anticipation of the management challenges you are likely to encounter as you implement STEM K–16 systemic reform. These include: trust, quality, and accountability.

*Depth*: There are two management issues relating to depth: (1) depth of science and mathematics content to advance the teaching and learning process—do pre-service and in-service K–12 teachers in your state have sufficient science and mathematics content knowledge to bring pupils to high levels of achievement?; and (2) engagement of consequential numbers of mathematicians, scientists, and teachers to determine impact. In many ways, depth is the tipping point where a project becomes institutionalized.

*Sustainability*: Consequential change must be continued and maintained over time in the face of competing demands, changing priorities, and teacher and administrator turnover.

*Spread*: There is one management issue relating to spread: the extent of "reach" or spread into school and university classrooms. Have you reached the point where changed practices are institutionalized in school and college classrooms? Are more schools and universities changing practices in their classrooms?

*Shift in Ownership*: Ownership for the changes must shift from the external impetus to the teachers, faculty, districts, schools, and universities who have the capacity to sustain, spread, and deepen the reform practices themselves.

*Trust*: The challenge is to build trust across K–12 and higher education cultures, acknowledging hierarchical differences, role differences within and across the two cultures, and between institutional cultures.

*Quality*: How do you ensure your K–16 STEM initiative is characterized by quality? Adhering to quality increases participation and results in attaining your intended outcomes. Inconsistent quality has the opposite effect.

*Accountability*: The management challenge is to find ways to enable each participating school and university to rise above characteristic behaviors of mere implementation, to examination, reflection, and transformation associated with evidence that positive outcomes have been obtained.

This chapter addresses how to bring your K–16 STEM initiative to scale. It reads from the perspective that you have already implemented various strategies as described in previous chapters. It suggests steps to be taken to sustain each strategy and to bring it to scale.

## CULTURE OF A SYSTEM

This book is about systemic change of a system. The system referred to is a large complex of education and support organizations that can be at the state, regional, or local levels. It ranges from the governing boards of K–12 and higher education institutions to a local school or college. It includes the parents and teachers in a school, the school system, faculty in science and mathematics departments, faculty in a college of education, principals, superintendents, college presidents, and so forth.

The culture of a system includes partnerships, policies, practices, and re-sources. Changing any one of these aspects of a system culture is to have changed its culture. One question is when and what brings a change to scale? To have changed a system's policy with respect to science and math-ematics, or a unit's science and mathematics pedagogy, or a unit's funding sources to support science and mathematics reform, is to have changed part of its culture—that is, only one aspect of its culture; this constitutes piece-meal change that might not be sustainable, rather than whole system change that is much more likely to be productive and sustainable.

An assessment and evaluation of cultural change must take into account alterations and modifications that involve the whole system rather than sim-ply its individual components. So, what is the evidence for whole system change, are there conditions when piecemeal changes are sustainable, and what actions need to be taken to bring and maintain changes?

In the *Tipping Point*, Gladwell (2000) provides a profoundly hopeful message that one imaginative person applying a well-placed lever can move the world. Are there little things that can make a large difference? Accord-ing to Gladwell, "This is the way social epidemics work." Change in owner-ship is one of the hallmarks advocated by Gladwell.

One way to rebuild America's competitive advantage in science and mathematics is to take or change ownership of the issue through a series of interrelated partnerships. Sustainability of effective partnerships goes a long way toward bringing a reform effort to scale. However, while a part-nership has an advocacy and management role to play in bringing a reform initiative to scale, it is the strategies or parts of them that have to be brought to scale.

Gladwell states three rules of the *Tipping Point*—the law of the few, the stickiness factor, and the power of context. Gladwell notes, "The power of context says that human beings are a lot more sensitive to their environ-ment than they may seem." For education reform, this means that context in each school building or on college campus must be recognized and strategies that work in the local context and not "one-size-fits-all" should be designed if they are going to be sustainable. For example, in chapter 6, this was found to be particularly true for implementation of well-functioning professional learning communities, or in chapter 7 for the *Work in the Schools* policy on various college campuses.

According to Gladwell, "The stickiness factor says that there are specific ways of making a contagious message memorable; there are relatively sim-ple changes in the presentation and structuring of information that can make a big difference in how much impact it makes." In chapter 4, a powerful slogan *Math + Science = Success* was found to resonate well with students and parents.

The law of the few says that an exceptional person can spread a trend through social connections and energy and enthusiasm and personality. As demonstrated in chapter 2, the Partnership for Reform In Science and Mathematics (PRISM) Leadership Team and its ability to spread reform through their various contacts at state, regional, and local levels is a good example of the law of the few.

## PARTNERSHIP SUSTAINABILITY

You have developed a coordinating state-level K–16 partnership team that is essential to ensure synergy of policy, resources, and structure. State K–12 leaders and state-level higher education leaders have agreed to form the alliance. To ensure that reforms are brought to scale, it is important for this alliance to meet on a regular basis and to include the right members. Individual members need to be of sufficient stature that they can represent their organization to the alliance and vice versa. In order to sustain the work of the alliance, it is necessary for partners to respect the contributions of one another and to commit to a shared vision of ensuring that all students have access to, are prepared for, and are encouraged to participate and succeed in challenging science and mathematics courses.

In addition to an alliance of state K–16 leaders, you have established a well-operating leadership team that coordinates the ongoing implementation of a set of interrelated strategies. This leadership team has a management role to ensure that the work is brought to scale. To succeed, it is important for your leadership team to attend to the four management challenges described in the introduction to this chapter: trust, quality, depth, and accountability.

At the state and local levels, robust K–16 partnerships have to be nurtured. At the local levels, your partnerships should include three-way collaborations among college science and mathematics faculty, science and mathematics education faculty, and teachers responsible for science and mathematics in the school districts that partner with the college.

Students are responsible for their own learning with the degree of responsibility increasing as they mature from kindergarten through college. However, regardless of the education level, teachers and faculty are expected to create learning conditions in which all students can learn.

Isolated actions taken by individuals might have impact on some students but it takes a set of coordinated actions to have a profound impact on many students. Thus, a lasting effect only occurs if the separate suggestions for actions for bringing to scale to be taken by various groups are integrated.

For depth, it is important for partners to be committed to a shared vision and goals to improve learning for their students. Your leadership team should hold one another accountable for achieving these shared goals. Decisions should be based on evidence gathered by the partners. When inconsistent quality is identified, it is critically important for your leadership team to take action, even when the situation is difficult. The old adage that a chain is only as strong as its weakest link applies to partnerships.

Sustainability is enhanced when partnerships attend to themselves as a partnership. The measurement tools and rubrics described in chapter 2 may be useful. Also, it is important for partners to report back to their individual institutions periodically on progress made toward common goals of the institutions and partnerships. You need to make sure such regular communication occurs, in particular to ensure continuity of an institution's participation in the probable event of a change in the individual representing the institution or the partnership.

For reach or spread, nothing beats success and communicating and rewarding success. You can engage consequential numbers of science and mathematics faculty, education faculty, and teachers in K–16 partnerships by trumpeting the successes of the initial local partnerships. While it is important to note the context in which a local partnership is achieving success, nonetheless the partnership tools are designed to encourage flexibility in meeting student success goals. As elaborated on in a later section, it is important to recognize and reward faculty and teachers for their contributions to student success.

While it is necessary to have a state leadership team to coordinate overall strategies and policies for student success, the more that a local partnership owns the initiative, the more the initiative thrives. Again, in order to encourage local partnerships, it is crucial that you recognize and reward faculty and teachers for their contributions to student success.

Whether at the state, regional, or local level, for sustainability, it is important to adhere to the five core principles described in chapter 2 to build strong and lasting partnerships.

*Partnerships require continuous attention*: The necessary time and resources must be invested toward a continual process of partnership development, including training and ongoing assessment.

*Leadership must be shared*: It is important for you to form and maintain a leadership triad, working as equals and developing trust in and respect for each other. The three-way collaboration of arts and sciences faculty, education faculty, and K–12 teachers is critical to your success.

*Partners must be given flexibility to accomplish project goals*: Flexibility is important on how to meet project goals so that partners can concurrently work toward individual goals.

*Decisions must be data-driven:* At all levels, a process of ongoing formative assessment is needed to improve your partnerships. There are a variety of measurement tools available for your use in evaluating your partnerships' attributes. Continued use of them should lead to sustainable changes that strengthen your partnerships.

*Communication is critical*: Collaboration is built on good communication. It is important for partnerships to include overlapping levels of leadership in order to build consensus and to foster understanding. Communication is ensured if partners work as equals and develop trust in and respect for each other.

## Partnership Management Tools

The state leadership team in your state has a management role to play to ensure that the work is brought to scale. On an annual basis, it is useful for your leadership team to rate itself on features and dimensions of partnerships and sustainability—see chapter 2. A useful strategy is for each participating region in your K–16 STEM initiative to complete the regional sections, as well. Ratings start with "no progress" and move to "sustained" across scales that measure a practice from "emerging" to "change institutionalized." Results can be used by the state and regions to determine where progress is being made and sustained, as well as where additional emphasis needs to be placed in order to achieve your goals.

*Use of Sustainability Rating to Demonstrate PRISM Progress.* An analysis of the combined ratings for four years of PRISM (ratings did not begin until year two) demonstrated a substantial decrease each year in the "no-progress" rating, with increases in the "sustained" rating.[2]

The partnership has been able to define clearly their roles and responsibilities in order to make hard decisions when needed. The partnership has been able to support the work of all PRISM partners sharing progress on PRISM goals periodically with the Georgia Department of Education and

Table 9.1.    Results of Sustainability Section of PRISM Management Tools

| Year | No Progress | In Progress | Met | Sustained |
|------|-------------|-------------|-----|-----------|
| Year 2 | 25.0% | 59.4% | 15.6% | 0.0% |
| Year 3 | 3.2% | 74.2% | 16.1% | 6.5% |
| Year 4 | 0.0% | 54.8% | 25.4% | 19.8% |
| Year 5 | 0.0% | 34.4% | 18.8% | 46.9% |

University System of Georgia, as well through regional and local entities. Partners continue to experiment with ways to redirect non-NSF resources toward PRISM efforts and goals.

## Professional Learning Communities

You have initiated K–16 professional learning communities and found that they are a successful form of local partnerships that provide a mechanism to sustain ongoing improvements in effective instruction—see chapter 6. To sustain them, it is important to continue to find ways to be flexible with teacher and faculty schedules allowing them enough time to fully participate in school-based or college-based learning communities.

There are three primary categories of knowledge about teaching that are normally considered: pedagogical content knowledge, ways of knowing in the discipline, and disciplinary content knowledge. No one category of teacher content knowledge is proposed as the only one that matters. Few would argue that any one of them is unimportant for teaching. In the local partnerships, especially in the professional learning communities, for sustainability it is important to ensure that pedagogical skill, teacher craft knowledge, and science and mathematics disciplinary knowledge are honored equally. Professional learning communities should include teachers and faculty who bring different depths of expertise from each of the three areas. Working as equals and developing trust and respect for each other is a hallmark of the sustainability of a successful partnership.

For sustainability, highly collaborative regional teams with representation from both higher education and K–12 schools are critical to providing support to learning community facilitators, enhancing communication, and coordinating learning community efforts at a regional level. It is also important for this team to be an ongoing resource for both K–16 professional learning communities and their individual members. Within this network of learning communities, each works toward a common overarching goal but maintains autonomy to establish its own vision and focus on specific individual needs. To sustain them, it is important to bring this network of local and regional learning communities together periodically to share lessons learned with each other and to evaluate collective progress.

Again, for sustainability, it is important to ensure that the work of the learning community members, both K–12 and higher education, is recognized, valued, and counted toward professional enhancement and advancement. It is likewise important to provide venues to celebrate publicly and showcase success and impact of professional learning community work. Not only does this add to sustainability of the particular learning community being showcased, but also it can add impetus to establishment of additional K–16 professional learning communities, thus contributing to bringing the efforts to scale.

## POLICY CHANGE

In order to sustain education reform, state-level policies that advocate for and encourage college faculty to be involved with their K–12 colleagues is critical. Such a policy was discussed in chapter 7.

Another needed state-level policy is one that addresses the most effective way to prepare future teachers by engaging arts and sciences faculty in teacher preparation and by providing true clinical preparation through cooperation between colleges of education and local schools. One approach to follow is to adopt a state-level policy that changes the governance structure for teacher preparation from a college of education to a three-way structure involving a college of education, a college of arts and sciences, and partner schools.

A third policy needed is State Board of Education approval of a K–12 curriculum framework that provides all students with a solid understanding of science and mathematics and prepares them with the knowledge and skills expected of them in high school that clearly align with expectations of college and work. If not already present in your state, it is necessary for it to be put in place. Also, it is important for school district policies to be developed that support participation of teachers and principals in activities such as K–16 professional learning communities.

Achieving a change in policy at the state level is difficult, but sustaining it should be relatively easy. The more difficult part is ensuring that practices are changed at the local levels of schools and colleges to be consistent with the policy changes. More of this is discussed in the next section on practices and activities change.

## PRACTICES AND ACTIVITIES CHANGE

### Supporting the K-12 Curriculum

Partnerships take many forms. A robust partnership is needed for development of the K-12 state curriculum in science and mathematics that includes teachers and faculty and K-12 and higher education administrators. It is important for this partnership to be responsible for ongoing improvements in the state's standards, instruction, and assessment. Having higher education as members of the partnership ensures a higher probability of alignment between K-12 end-of-course and graduation examinations and placement tests in higher education. Such alignment is necessary for higher student success in college.

For depth, it is important to ascertain that K-12 courses and curricula are designed to bring students to a "meets standards level or above" on state and national assessments. While this is a necessary step, it is not sufficient. The challenges are to ensure that all students take and complete appropriate challenging science and mathematics courses and teachers are able to bring all students to high levels of achievement in science and mathematics.

Similarly, for sustainability, it is important for your STEM initiative to have reach or spread in local school districts. Members of your regional partnerships from K-12 and higher education groups working with teachers and leaders on curriculum development, that parallels the efforts at the state level, is one way to do this. These groups can facilitate teacher examination of student data and their use in a continual process of reflection, evaluation, and revision of the local curricula.

To maximize the extent of reach of your K-16 STEM initiative into school classrooms, it is important for your state- and regional-level partnerships to work continuously on development of assignments, inquiry-based teaching and learning, and assessment. Such work should include knowledge of areas of student difficulty related to particular science and mathematics concepts. Achieving depth to ensure that all students take challenging science and mathematics courses is addressed below in the section on enhancing public awareness.

Sustainability of curricular change at the state level requires the commitment of state K-12 leaders to hold regular substantive meetings of the group that is responsible for ongoing improvements in the state's standards, instruction, and assessment. Similarly, for sustainability at the school-district level, K-12 leaders need to commit to support groups working on curriculum development.

For spread or reach, it is important for school leaders to ensure that teachers in local school districts have the time necessary to work with peers to improve their practice. Teachers should be encouraged to make use of professional learning opportunities that have a focus on strategies such as inquiry-based teaching and learning, differentiated instruction, contextual teaching and learning, conceptual change, and problem-based learning.

## Improving Learning in College Courses

Introducing science and mathematics faculty to active learning strategies through institutes or academies for learning and providing incentives such as a small grants program has the potential to increase students' interest, proficiency, and success in science and mathematics and to increase science and quantitative literacy for students—see chapter 7.

Improving learning in introductory courses is one area where structure is important. For sustainability of work underway, some kind of institute or other entity is needed that can bring faculty together to learn, share, research, and document effective practices of cognitive sciences and practitioners in teaching and learning science and mathematics. Many campuses have a center for teaching and learning or equivalent entity. The first action higher education faculty and administrators may wish to take to bring the changes to scale is to establish a learning center, if one does not already exist.

If a teaching and learning center is already in place, it is important for staff to have the expertise needed to be able to help science and mathematics faculty with action research strategies and instruments to measure changes in instructional practices. Such a center can provide faculty a forum to discuss, within and across disciplinary boundaries, the multitude of active learning strategies that are successful in other institutions. Part of the issue of little improvement in student success in introductory science and mathematics courses is a lack of awareness by instructors of many learning strategies that have proved to be successful nationally. Establishment of a learning center is an important first step.

For depth, it is important to ask if the active learning strategies are embodied in a way that faculty engage students in using materials and tasks. It's one thing to learn about some strategy in a workshop, but how is the strategy being applied in the classroom and does its application result in increased student learning? Through institutes or other similar events, faculty strengthen their skills in collecting and analyzing data on student learning, and have opportunities to share their insights with colleagues.

As an example, faculty working together using techniques derived from Japanese Lesson Study can reinforce one another in refining strategies for overcoming students' difficulties with concepts or misconceptions—see chapter 6.

If you find that faculty modeling effective active learning strategies leads to deeper student understanding, then how do you measure that such changes in instructional practices are brought to scale? And how do you ensure that the changes persist over time? For sustainability, it is important for instruments used to measure changes in instructional practice to include questions, such as: Are active learning strategies becoming the norm for the involved faculty? Have these faculty moved progressively from including more active learning strategies in a single course to using more active learning strategies in all their courses? In this way, your actions can track changes over time and allow you to determine sustainability at the individual faculty-member level.

Actions you can take to encourage reach or spread include keeping department chairs and other senior faculty leaders informed of progress in improvement in courses. In particular, you could ask them to include introductory courses in science and mathematics for discussion at department meetings and retreats since these courses generally enroll the largest number of students and increases in student confidence, interest, and learning can have a positive influence on the number of students who become STEM majors. When local successes are obtained, not only should the responsible faculty be recognized, but also the department should encourage moving from one or a few instructors to all instructors in introductory courses using the effective learning strategies. In this way, the underlying beliefs and practices can spread to other faculty in the department.

Some additional questions you can ask in instruments to measure changes in instructional practice are: Do the underlying beliefs and practices spread to other faculty in the department? Has a department moved from one or a few instructors to all instructors in introductory courses using effective learning strategies? Is there an impact on reward, recognition, and incentive policies in the department?

Another possible action to encourage spread is to advocate not only for recognition for responsible faculty but also for department policies and practices that provide incentives and rewards for contributions to enhanced student learning.

At the institution or college level, actions that administrators can take to encourage higher education faculty to learn new effective approaches to teaching and then apply them include those suggested by a National Research Council (1999) panel. Establishment of a centralized fund for education improvement in the provost or dean's office can send a powerful message regarding a change in departmental values. Provosts and deans advocating for the use of effective course designs and assessments in courses can help to change the culture on campus.

## Involving College Faculty in K–12 Activities

Once you have determined the interests of college faculty in K–12 activities by strategies such as those discussed in chapter 7, you can introduce them through professional learning communities or regional institutes and provide incentives such as a small grants program to encourage their involvement in K–12 activities. The professional learning community model (see chapter 6) is a powerful way to bring together higher education faculty and K–12 teachers to work collectively on improving K–16 STEM teaching and student learning.

Similar to the above section on improving learning in college courses, college faculty may need assistance in conducting action research if they are to use assessment to improve learning in either their own or in K–12 classrooms. For depth, it is important to ask if involvement of college faculty in K–12 activities is leading to modifications employed in the classrooms that result in improved student learning. It's one thing to discuss a strategy in a professional learning community, but is the strategy being applied in the classroom and does it result in increased student learning?

For the sustained involvement of higher education faculty with K–12 schools, the faculty reward system needs to change—see chapter 7. Are there incentives in place to encourage and reward the faculty members? Are faculty being recognized for their contributions to areas that are a departure from current disciplinary conventions? Does this newly valued work actually count in annual merit increases or promotions?

Actions that can be taken to encourage reach or spread are similar to those discussed above in the section on improving learning in college courses, such as keeping department chairs and leaders informed of successes that result from involvement of college faculty in K–12 activities and advocating for recognition in policies and practices. Through such advocacy, there should be a slight shift in ownership as more college faculty become involved in meaningful K–12 activities. A key to such a positive development lies in the next section.

## Changes in Faculty Roles and Rewards System

The National Research Council (1999) panel offers another recommendation for provosts and deans to advocate for policies and practices in promotion, tenure, and salary deliberations that reward documented faculty work that engages students in courses or by advocating for research focused on teaching and learning the discipline as evidence of a faculty member's productivity as a teacher-scholar.

Other measures of shift in reform ownership include following along two dimensions—within an institution and across institutions in a state. At this point, it is probably beyond actions that individual faculty can take. Nevertheless, within an institution, administrators and senate leaders can take actions to ensure that policies and practices for faculty roles and rewards are being changed to recognize that improved learning in courses could, with documented evidence, count as a scholarly contribution instead of a teaching contribution.

For faculty roles and rewards, how do you measure that changes in the reward system are being brought to scale? Is there a change in the breadth of what is rewarded? For example, is it possible for work in the schools to count as a scholarly contribution instead of a service contribution? Do changes persist over time? Are the president, provost, dean and department chairs in arts and sciences, and dean and department chairs in education actively advocating for such changes? Is there an impact on reward, recognition, and incentive policies and practices in the department? Are increasing numbers of arts and sciences and education faculty incorporating work in the schools and improvement of courses into their workload?

There are a number of ways that you can gauge progress on changes in a faculty roles and rewards system. Some potential leading indicators that could be monitored include: Is support via financial resources, such as small grants, being made available to appropriate offices on campus to support involvement of faculty with K–12 schools or in improvement of college courses, especially those that involve future teachers? Are increasing numbers of arts and sciences and education faculty incorporating this type of work in their workload? Do institutions have in place policies and programs to recognize and reward faculty for this work?

You could include some potential lagging indicators such as, for advocacy, within arts and sciences and education: Do faculty have a clear understanding as to what constitutes "significance" in scholarly teaching, in the scholarship of teaching and learning, and in the scholarship of engagement? Do increased numbers of faculty in arts and sciences and education draw upon the available financial resources to increase their involvement in this type of work?

Do increasing numbers of arts and sciences and education faculty generate products and deliverables as a direct result of their participation in the teaching, scholarship, and service activities? Are increasing numbers of faculty recognized and rewarded for significant participation in approved efforts on teacher preparation and school improvement through decisions in promotion and tenure, pre-tenure, post-tenure review, annual review, merit pay, and workload?

Beyond an institution, state higher education leaders can ask if changes in practices in some institutions are being adopted more widely in other institutions.

## Instructional Practices—In-Service Teachers

Professional learning is the key to improving teacher quality, but only if it is planned systematically in relation to the goals of the school or district. It can change the culture of the school from one where teachers make decisions haphazardly and in isolation of their colleagues to one where the whole school focus is on instructional decisions that improve student learning. In order to accomplish and sustain this type of culture change, it is important for teacher professional learning to be designed using a collaborative team process involving support staff, administrators, university faculty, and teachers.

Effective and sustainable teacher professional learning requires explicit learning outcomes, collaborative partnerships, and improved instructional strategies and resources. The three principles to keep in mind as you plan and implement are: (1) professional learning should integrate content and pedagogy, (2) professional learning design should be guided by cognitive research on learning and rely upon research-based instructional practices, and (3) professional learning should be aligned to individual, school, and district needs. A collaborative professional learning culture focused on achieving higher levels of student learning in science and mathematics prepares K–16 educators to meet the STEM challenge.

To sustain continued professional growth, it is important for teachers to assess regularly themselves using an instrument such as *Inventory of Teaching and Learning (ITAL)*, which was introduced in chapter 8. The *ITAL* instrument allows teachers to make judgments relative to the emphasis they place on about fifty classroom practices. They choose a rating that best reflects the degree of emphasis they typically give to each practice. Part of the instrument's value lies in raising the awareness of teachers to various effective practices. They can use the ratings to guide themselves on areas where they would like additional help and development. Another value is that they can chart their own progress.

A useful way to drive towards institutionalizing change is by asking K–12 teachers to reflect on and assess their teaching towards the desired result of increased student learning in science and mathematics. When teachers collect and analyze data on student learning as a measure of their teaching effectiveness and when they make decisions about which approaches work and why and share their insights with peers in venues such as professional learning communities, then you have brought about systemic change.

## Instructional Practices—Pre-service Teachers

The teacher pipeline also needs attention. It is important for future teachers in your state to be prepared by programs that are the shared responsibility of education faculty, arts and sciences faculty, and classroom teachers in the schools. When working together the three groups are better positioned to: (1) define and ensure the subject-matter competence of all teacher candidates; (2) ensure that all teacher candidates can make the connections between subject-matter knowledge and the learning needs of children; and (3) ensure that all teacher candidates can promote student learning within the realities of the classroom.

It is important that all your faculty members involved with teacher preparation, including instructors of introductory college courses, are knowledgeable of and employ strategies to engage students in their learning. One way to do this is to provide college faculty, especially from science and mathematics, a venue to learn about such strategies. Examples were given earlier in chapter 7 through either regional or statewide institutes or through regional or statewide academies for learning.

## Students and Parents

Research findings indicate that parents and guardians are key influencers of their children. As noted in chapter 4, student achievement improves when parents become involved in their children's education at school and in the community. At a minimum, it is important to include in your K–16 STEM initiative Math and Science Family Nights that bring parents to the school to participate in science and mathematics activities with their children. Chapter 4 elaborates on some incentives and models for successfully encouraging parental participation.

To achieve depth of parental involvement, it is important to ascertain that the family night events caused some changes in parental attitudes about their role in supporting their child's science and mathematics education, and whether their awareness increased as to the importance of science and mathematics for their children. To do this, you can use questionnaires at the beginning and end of the school year. In addition, you can gauge changes in student motivation and student achievement in science and mathematics.

For example, student motivation could be measured using subscales of the MSP-Motivation Assessment Project (Karabenick and Maehr 2008) scales. In particular, three of the subscales are appropriate to assess student motivation: (1) Task Value Beliefs—student beliefs about the utility and importance of science and mathematics as an area of study, (2) Interest—a student's attraction to, liking for, and enjoyment of science and mathematics, and (3) Achievement Goals—some goals focus on learning and understanding, while others focus on demonstrating ability. These instruments could be administered to students by their regular classroom teachers.

If you have a broad-based public awareness campaign in place, it is important to target your messages to parents and guardians. Parents or guardians influence student behavior by encouraging and supporting their achievement in science and mathematics. To have any impact, your message must be memorable.

To achieve depth of impact on parents and guardians, you need to ascertain that the public awareness campaign caused some changes in their attitudes about their role in supporting their child's science and mathematics education. This can be accomplished by surveys conducted at regular intervals in the school districts that are targeted in the campaign. The most effective way to target schools is to use a combination of campaign materials and family night events.

For sustainability, data need to be gathered on whether or not school districts incorporate Math and Science Family Nights into their yearly calendar of events at all schools. If campaign materials are used, it is also important to obtain data on the impact of these materials.

Actions you can take to encourage spread or reach to additional school districts include keeping superintendents and other statewide education leaders informed of progress in improvement of student attitudes, motivation, and achievements in science and mathematics in the school districts that encourage more parental involvement. When successes occur in such school districts, local school leaders should be recognized and their public and businesses made aware of the importance of parental and community involvement.

Shifting ownership from educators to a shared responsibility among educators, parents and guardians, and the community, especially businesses and corporations, more likely occurs with successful demonstration of the positive impact of greater parental involvement. It also makes it easier to interest corporations in participating in a Public Awareness Campaign.

The development of a broad-based Public Awareness Campaign requires a great deal of resources coupled with committed partners who are willing to define and refine target audience messages. For sustainability, at regular intervals, data must be collected and monitored to make sure the campaign goals are reached and that there is evidence that the campaign has had some resulting and measurable effect on the attitudes and perceptions you hope to change.

Bringing to scale in a state probably requires a statewide Public Awareness Campaign. To generate funding to assist with such a campaign, you could seek corporations using various co-branded collateral items to suggest their support of STEM education and statewide efforts to encourage student interest in the field. Various options in which corporations could join the Public Awareness Campaign efforts can range from receiving less significant exposure to quite noticeable exposure based on the needs of the corporation. As you look for new corporations to approach, it is important to make sure corporate dollars work for sustainability efforts and programs that look to influence student and parent choice.

## Evaluation

You have established an ongoing evaluation of the work of your partnership and determined data to be gathered and instruments for gathering the data. It is important to analyze regularly the data and provide ongoing feedback to the state, regional, or local leadership teams. It is important not only to share formative and yearly evaluation reports with regional and state leaders but also to provide a formal mechanism for leaders to respond to evaluation reports. In particular, monthly meetings of your evaluation team are important with the participation of your overall STEM project director.

For depth, it is necessary to ascertain that data being gathered and analyzed are appropriate for furtherance of the goals of increased student learning. For example, while you might collect information that participants meet regularly in professional learning communities, this does not necessarily mean that the partners are deepening their knowledge of what works for their students or that they are applying such knowledge when they return to their classrooms. Instruments are needed that probe the use of increased knowledge that results from the meetings.

Sustainability at the state, regional, or local levels occurs naturally if you adopt the practice of featuring review of data as part of your regular meetings. Regular reviews have the added benefit of a shift in ownership of the data from something for which the evaluation team is responsible to every partner being involved with the data.

Actions you can take to encourage spread or reach of effective practices in evaluation include keeping team leaders at the state, regional, and local levels aware of the various instruments and analyses that are being used and the positive results that emanate from such usage.

However, staying flexible enough to change your plan or add different data-collection strategies or instruments as the project evolves over multiple years is key to success and sustainability. The evaluation team must be a true partnership, with qualitative and quantitative evaluators continually identifying ways their strategies and resulting data support the other in broadening and giving more depth of understanding about effectiveness of reform strategies in STEM education. The evaluation team must also function in a truly collaborative fashion with the project leadership.

## Changes in Institutional and State-Level Support and Resources

Documentation of your successes as your K–16 STEM initiative progresses helps to increase the likelihood of availability of resources to sustain your work. An example of a state investment is the STEM initiative of the University System of Georgia (USG). This initiative represents one of the better ways of bringing to scale the successes of a K–16 STEM initiative through a continuing investment by a state.

*University System of Georgia STEM Initiative.*   In 2007, the USG chancellor noted

> Georgia must respond to the increasing state and national crises in the education of mathematicians, scientists, technicians and engineers and the preparation of teachers in these fields. Addressing the need to increase the number of baccalaureate degrees in these fields is one of the highest priorities of the University System of Georgia.
>
> Accordingly, I have committed to the provision of funding to support the successful implementation of our *Math + Science = Success* Initiative over the next several years. As outlined in the STEM (Science, Technology, Engineering, and Mathematics) Report, we are providing an immediate $1.6 million to launch this initiative and we are preparing to add $3.6 million per year beginning in 2009.
>
> This investment alone will not achieve our goal of dramatically increasing the number of baccalaureate degrees awarded in Georgia in STEM disciplines nor greatly increase the number of teachers prepared to work in our schools.

Part of this investment will be funds that you may apply for to increase the capacity of your institution to reach new targets. However, this initiative is also designed to encourage and support your review of institutional capacity to accommodate more students in these fields, improve the quality of teaching in critical courses, and enable larger number of students to succeed in these fields. Institutions must also examine their own capacity to redirect investments within to address the goals found in this document within the scope of your missions.

Accordingly, beginning in FY 2008, I'm adding the following criteria to the annual evaluations of all USG presidents: (1) Percent of students who earn a grade of C or better, and the percent who withdraw, in the following introductory courses, compared to the previous year:

- Math Modeling, College Algebra, Pre-Calculus.
- Introductory Biology Courses for majors and non-majors.
- Introductory Chemistry Courses for majors and non-majors.

(2) Annual institutional targets set for the number of baccalaureate degrees in STEM fields and results toward achieving the targets (if applicable to mission).

(3) Annual institutional targets set for the number of new science and mathematics teachers to be prepared for middle school and high school and results toward achieving the targets (if applicable to mission).

The University System of Georgia thus encourages its institutions to invest in effective STEM practices. It reinforces these practices by requiring presidents to be aware of some of their institutions' key data on success of college students in science and mathematics courses and programs. Thus the STEM initiative should go a long way toward bringing to scale a statewide reform in K–16 education.

Part of the STEM initiative provides resources for institutions to encourage scientists and mathematicians and science and mathematics education faculty to collaborate in K–16 learning communities and for science and mathematics faculty to work on increasing student understanding in introductory science and mathematics courses. Another part is funding to provide a state-level Institute on the Teaching and Learning of Science and Mathematics throughout the USG that focuses on teaching college introductory courses in mathematics and the sciences. All institutions that offer the associate or baccalaureate degree are eligible to participate. Through this institute, faculty members explore use of new teaching methods that have been shown to be effective, while maintaining high standards and expectations.

## Advisory Committees

Advisory committees at the state level provide significant impetus to reform in K–16 education. In order to sustain statewide reform, it is important to ensure that relevant committees are active and ongoing. Of particular importance are K–16 committees such as the ones discussed in chapter 3. For example, in an effort to provide teachers with tasks, student work, and commentary intended to illustrate the standards, instructional frameworks at every grade level and for each high school course can be updated and revised by collaborative teams of K–12 teachers and higher education faculty.

## FINDINGS AND LESSONS LEARNED

What have we found to be most challenging issues in our work? An analysis of our scoring on the sustainability management tools reveals that after five years we are still in progress on a number of items. In particular, it is exceedingly difficult to change teacher reward systems and to have current teachers recognized for their important roles and responsibilities in the preparation of aspiring teachers as well as in their own continued professional development. It also continues to be a work in progress on changing practices at the level of college departments.

## NOTES

1. Ronald J. Henry is the co-principal investigator in the Partnership for Reform In Science and Mathematics (PRISM), a systemic K–16 STEM initiative in Georgia. He is a physicist and the provost and senior vice president for Academic Affairs at Georgia State University in Atlanta.

2. The management tools are on pages 14–26 of http://www.gaprism.org/presentations/reports/2008/tools_manage_projects.pdf.

# 10

# SUMMARY OF STEPS
# NECESSARY FOR SUCCESS

*Sheila Jones, Janet S. Kettlewell, and Ronald J. Henry*[1]

## INTRODUCTION

This book is about state and local partnerships of schools, colleges, and policy leaders engaging in systemic improvements in K–16 education, in order to rebuild America's competitive advantage in science, technology, engineering, and mathematics (STEM). Each chapter includes specific strategies for how you can develop or extend a STEM initiative in your state into one that is systemic and one that impacts the education of students at all levels of the education spectrum—school through college.

Chapter 1 lays out a framework for systemic K–16 STEM initiatives and suggests as a starting point an in-depth analysis of work already underway in your state. The design, then, for your K–16 STEM initiative can be derived from taking stock of work already underway and from analyses of your data as to where improvements are needed most.

Chapter 2 offers concrete steps for development of robust partnerships that are essential for successful systemic K–16 reform in STEM. Chapter 3 provides you with suggestions for putting in place strong sets of science and mathematics K–12 curricular standards and connecting your K–16 STEM initiative to that state work. In addition, chapter 3 helps you engage higher education in the process of K–12 curriculum development in science and mathematics so that the knowledge and skills expected of students in high school clearly align with expectations for college and work. The crucial role of parents and guardians in influencing their children is a major theme of chapter 4.

Many ideas for enhancing instructional practices for in-service and pre-service teachers are provided in chapters 5, 6, and 7. Chapter 5 also delineates an approach to changing the professional development culture for K–12 teachers. Chapter 6 explains how K–16 professional learning communities can help you sustain and accelerate the content and pedagogical knowledge of K–12 science and mathematics teachers and the pedagogical knowledge of scientists and mathematicians in higher education. Particular actions that can be taken to ensure the sustainable participation of STEM higher education faculty in your initiative are emphasized in chapter 7.

In chapter 8, you learn how to design and implement a comprehensive evaluation and how evaluation can be used to promote continuous improvement and sustainability. Chapter 9 includes specific strategies to ensure the sustainability of your systemic K–16 STEM initiative, once underway.

While each chapter in this book describes major components of a coherent K–16 systemic STEM initiative, it is important to recognize that all must be emphasized to optimize success. The particular emphasis you give to each strategy should be guided by your assessment of work already underway in your state and by your analysis of your K–16 student achievement data.

In Georgia, for example, just prior to beginning the PRISM K–16 initiative, major work had been completed on the preparation of pre-service science and mathematics teachers in the University System of Georgia. So, that work was built upon in our STEM initiative rather than featured within the initiative. If major work in STEM is already underway in your state, then a recommended strategy is to add any pieces that may be missing after your review of this book.

This chapter pulls together for the reader a summary of all the steps and actions described in previous chapters to help you ensure that connections are optimized among the various strategies in your systemic K–16 STEM initiative. The authors hope that the review of these steps by readers in your state will help unite the energy and commitments of key partners toward building a sustainable K–16 STEM initiative that results in increased student learning and achievement in STEM fields in schools and colleges.

## REVIEW OF STEPS NEEDED FOR A SUCCESSFUL K–16 STEM INITIATIVE

This book lays out actions that can be taken by K–12 and higher education faculty and administrators, and state policy makers, to implement a systemic

K–16 STEM initiative. Following each of the steps from previous chapters, which are summarized below, will increase your probability for success.

## Step 1. Taking Stock in Your State

Four categories of questions are offered that when answered should help you establish the major strategies in the design of your systemic K–16 STEM initiative:

### K–12 Curriculum

- Does your state have rigorous science and mathematics standards in place?
- Are four core academic science and mathematics courses required of all students to graduate high school?
- Are core science and mathematics courses (for all students) aligned with expectations for college and careers?
- Do students meet or exceed your state science and mathematics standards?

### Higher Education Curriculum

- What are student success rates (grades of A, B, or C) in introductory science and mathematics courses in your state?
- How many students in your state arrive at college believing they want to be STEM majors and change their minds after taking introductory science and mathematics courses?
- Do college faculty in your state see a connection between their teaching practices and student success rates in introductory science and mathematics courses?
- Do student persistence and graduation rates in STEM fields meet or exceed national averages?

### Student Interest

- Do you know if, and at what grade level, students in your state lose interest in STEM?
- Do you know who in your state has the greatest influence over student course-taking patterns in science and mathematics?
- Are there programs in place in your state to increase student interest in becoming scientists and mathematicians?
- Are there programs in place in your state to increase student interest in becoming science and mathematics teachers?

## Teaching—In Schools and Colleges

- How many elementary teachers in your state have sufficient content knowledge in science and mathematics?
- How many middle grades teachers are teaching science and mathematics with less than an academic minor in the field?
- How many high school teachers are teaching mathematics, biology, chemistry, or physics with less than an academic major in the field?
- How many instructors teaching college introductory science and mathematics courses and labs are not able to speak English sufficiently for students to understand them?

## Incentives for K–12 Teachers and Higher Education Faculty

- Are financial incentives in place in your state for individuals to become science and mathematics teachers?
- Are financial incentives in place in your state for current teachers to strengthen their content knowledge in science and mathematics?
- Are incentives in place in your state for higher education faculty to be rewarded through promotion, tenure, and salary, for collaborative work with K–12 schools?
- Can such K–16 work count within their workload?

## Step 2. Develop Strong Partnerships

All partners must be committed to shared leadership while investing in the time necessary to work collaboratively. Partners must be willing to hold one another accountable for achieving the goals and objectives of your K–16 STEM initiative. Formative assessments are necessary to ensure a cycle of continuous improvement. Every partner must be willing to communicate from the top-down and the bottom-up. Five principles with actions steps (from chapter 2) are suggested to guide development of a successful partnership in your state or region.

*Principle 1: Partnerships require continuous attention.* It is important to establish a regular meeting schedule for your STEM partnership and to hold these meetings in a neutral site. Likewise, it is necessary for the team that is leading your K–16 STEM initiative to recognize that not all members of your team know how to collaborate. Training on partnership development may prove to be useful.

Once you begin implementation of your K–16 STEM design, it is very important to monitor your implementation plans regularly. If your experience mirrors ours, holding annual two-day retreats for your STEM leadership team to focus on long-term planning is helpful.

*Principle 2: Leadership must be shared.* School and college cultures differ significantly. Attention is needed to breaking down barriers between the two cultures. A way to do this is to ensure that you plan everything jointly—involving K–16 partners at every step. It is also important to make sure that you have the right people—policy leaders and opinion leaders—involved in the work.

*Principle 3: Partners must be given flexibility to accomplish project goals.* While it is necessary to keep the partnership structure transparent to all participants and to maintain a focus on common goals, it is also important to allow for differences among local partnerships. Not all regions have to go about reaching a goal in the same way. Honor their differences and avoid a cookie-cutter approach.

*Principle 4: Decisions must be data-driven.* From the very beginning it is important for your STEM K–16 leadership team to make sure that all decisions are based on data—even decisions about your partnership. In order to make data-driven decisions about your partnership, you may find that tools are not available. Chapter 2 includes several tools that you might find to be helpful. If they do not suit your purposes, you may need to develop new tools. Members of your evaluation team should be able to help you with both development of the tools and their use in monitoring your progress.

*Principle 5: Communication is critical.* It is important for your STEM leadership team to establish an avenue or mechanism for communicating with all partners. To optimize your effectiveness, at least part of your communication needs to take place in face-to-face meetings. During these meetings, it is important for all members of your STEM leadership team to listen to one another and to be open to exploring new ideas. Building trust and learning about both school and college cultures takes time, but it is time well spent.

### Step 3. Support the Design of a Challenging K–12 Science and Mathematics Curriculum

Development of state K–12 standards and curriculum in science and mathematics is the purview of the State Board of Education and the State Education Agency in each state. If K–12 curricular reform in science and mathematics is underway in your state, it is important for the K–16 leaders of your STEM initiative to connect in some way to the statewide improvements.

Higher education faculty participation in the development of K–12 science and mathematics curricular standards and course sequences can help your state to ensure that when students meet the standards and complete the course sequences, they are ready for college and work. Likewise, if higher education faculty are going to produce K–12 science and mathematics teachers who are able to teach to the standards set, they too must understand the K–12 curriculum.

Accordingly, the actions suggested for step three include those for State Boards of Education and State Departments of Education as well as those for K–16 STEM partners.

***For State Boards of Education and State Departments of Education.*** It is helpful to enlist external curriculum audits or reviews of your current K–12 science and mathematics standards by an independent organization and publicize results to draw attention to the need for curricular change. As the need is recognized, it is likewise important to have strong commitment and resolve from key policy makers with the authority to lead raising standards and expectations.

Creation of expert advisory panels is helpful when given the authority to review curriculum standards from other states, countries, and groups, and to develop a plan for developing new curriculum standards. It is important to invite the participation of higher education scientists and mathematicians in the development of new K–12 curricular standards and to receive feedback on the various drafts of standards from higher education STEM faculty in addition to that of teachers and the public.

It is important for new K–12 curricular standards in science and mathematics to be aligned with and benchmarked against national and international standards that are reputable, rigorous, and balanced. Partnership with national initiatives, such as the American Diploma Project, is highly recommended, which involves both K–12 and higher education communities in the standards development that will ensure all high school graduates are both college- and work-ready. The use of follow-up external audits and reviews of new curricular standards can help to build public trust and confidence in their quality.

***For the K–16 STEM Partners in Your State.*** It is critically important for your K–16 STEM leadership team to partner with your state education agency in development and implementation of new or revised K–12 standards in science and mathematics. Leaders of your K–16 STEM initiative can facilitate collaboration between college and university faculty and K–12 leaders and teachers in all stages of curriculum development.

Likewise, leaders of your K–16 STEM initiative can help with development of instructional frameworks and science and mathematics tools that are created collaboratively by K–12 teachers and higher education faculty for teachers. Your K–16 STEM leadership team can get involved in providing professional learning on the new curricular standards and in supporting teachers in their efforts to make the needed changes in instructional delivery and assessment. Finally, your K–16 STEM leadership team can support similar changes in the colleges and universities in your state to ensure that newly prepared science and mathematics teachers are ready to teach the K–12 students to the new standards.

### Step 4. Provide Opportunities to Engage K–12 Students and Their Parents so They Understand the Importance of STEM Courses and Careers, Including Teaching

The two examples provided in chapter 4 should help your partnership create the tools needed to inform parents, students, educators, and the community at-large as to the importance of all students taking and being successful in challenging science and mathematics courses. The action steps from chapter 4 that are necessary to implement a public awareness campaign and an academy for future teachers of science and mathematics are summarized here.

*Public Awareness Campaign.* A comprehensive communications plan includes message development, public relations, advertising and marketing, media placement, and a research and evaluation component. Inclusion of market research allows you to plan for relevant nuances in your various communities.

It is important to establish a campaign team to coordinate this work. Once assembled your campaign team can make sure that all parties understand the importance of testing and retesting your collateral materials with state and educational partners as well as with the intended audiences before you launch the campaign. Your campaign team needs to be ready and willing to make suggested changes—especially those that come from your target audiences.

It is important for your campaign team to carefully plan where, when, and how you showcase your advertising material. The campaign team should make sure that all developed materials can be used in a number of ways by several different audiences. Placement of your campaign materials on a Web site is highly recommended to spur interest and to expand your campaign beyond your immediate reach. Events, such as Math and Science Family Nights, help take your campaign to the level of increased engagement of both students and their parents.

Campaigns are costly. So it is important to find ways to connect with other organizations and corporations interested in helping you advance your efforts and the Campaign. In order to ensure that your costly campaign is effective, it is also important to make sure that it is a strategy embedded within your K–16 STEM initiative and not separate from it.

*Advanced Academy for Future Teachers (AAFT).*   When starting an AAFT program, it is best to find a school that has a background in providing students with career training and summer enrichment opportunities to expedite the eventual "launch" of your program. It is also necessary to partner with a college or university interested in a long-term commitment of developing a potential pipeline of students desiring teaching as a career in science or mathematics.

AAFT works best for rising and current eleventh and twelfth graders. Student recruitment into the program needs to start early and to be continuous. It is helpful to look for students who excel in science or mathematics as well as those who express interest in teaching and tutoring.

The program works best when you schedule concentrated sessions during the summer along with periodic meetings during the school year. Because AAFT is a summer-intensive program, and your audience is eleventh and twelfth graders, it is important to provide students with some kind of stipend and to pay their transportation costs because they will have to forego summer jobs in order to participate.

Since the goals of AAFT are to increase student interest in going to college and in becoming either science or mathematic teachers, it is important to select carefully the instructors for this program. Find school-year and summer instructors who have a passion for learning and teaching—instructors who enjoy working with students and who are eager to try untested styles and methods of instruction. Encourage instructors to include field trips and other outside-of-the-classroom experiences that enrich the program activities.

Finally, it is important for your K–16 STEM partnership to recognize the accomplishments of AAFT student participants. One way to do this is to hold ceremonial events at the end of the year to reward (and encourage) students for their hard work.

## Step 5. Enhance Instructional Practices for K–16 Educators

Professional development is the key to improving teaching quality at both the K–12 and higher education levels. While the strategies for enhancing instructional practices may differ, they are needed at all levels. K–16 professional learning communities are proving to be a very strong strategy for improving teaching and learning in science and mathematics in both schools and colleges. This step integrates the work described in chapters 5 and 6. Action steps are summarized here for building professional development for K–12 teachers and for implementing K–16 professional learning communities.

**Building Effective Professional Development for K–12 In-Service Teachers.**    It is important for K–16 STEM partnerships at the regional level to create or adopt a framework for guiding the design process for professional development of K–12 in-service science and mathematics teachers. If you do not have such a framework already in place, the one proposed by Loucks-Horsley et al. (2003) is recommended. This framework involves:

- Committing to a vision and standards,
- Analyzing student learning and other data,
- Setting goals by identifying critical issues,
- Planning the strategies to be used to accomplish the goals,
- Doing the professional development activity, and
- Evaluating the impact of the activity on teacher practice and student learning

It is also important for your K–16 STEM partnership to align professional development to your school or district needs. This can be done through use of data analysis to identify a focus for professional development.

Research-based practices that integrate content and pedagogy should be used in the design of professional development activities to accomplish your goals. It is important to consider contextual issues, such as teacher background, schedule, and place when designing the activities. It is equally important to involve community resources and higher education faculty partners early in the planning stages. As we all know, teachers tire quickly of "sit and git" sessions. So, don't be afraid to try new formats for professional learning.

Involve your teachers in their own professional development. On-site mathematics and science teaching experts can work with collaborative teacher teams and provide small group professional learning, in addition to working one-on-one with teachers in their classrooms. Targeting professional learning toward developing teacher leaders can help significantly in building teacher capacity.

**K–16 Professional Learning Communities.**    K–16 profession learning communities represent new work to both teachers and higher education faculty. It is, therefore, important to establish a highly collaborative regional team with representation from both higher education and K–12 schools to provide support to learning community facilitators, enhance communication, and coordinate learning community efforts at a regional level. This team should also be an ongoing resource for both K–16 professional learning communities and their individual members.

Featuring a network of K–16 professional learning communities in the design of your K–16 STEM initiative can be a useful way to support school-district and higher education participation. It involves several schools and colleges working toward a common overarching goal, but maintaining autonomy to focus individual learning community work on specific needs.

You should note that most K–16 professional learning communities need high-quality training. Not everyone knows how to be a good partner.

Likewise, significant numbers of K–12 teachers and higher education faculty need to be involved in designing regional K–16 professional learning community implementation plans and activities. The involvement of a critical mass of participants in the developmental stages of the partnership allows for participant ownership of the learning community structure and activities. Included in the developmental stages must be the collective determination of how success is to be measured and shared and how progress is to be assessed regularly as a group.

The availability of structured opportunities for K–16 professional learning communities to engage in collective learning, true collaboration, and shared practice can expedite progress. Part of the structure is the provision of venues to publicly celebrate and showcase success and impact of learning community work. For K–16 professional learning communities to reach their potential, it is necessary to ensure that the work of the learning community members, both K–12 and higher education, is recognized, valued, and counted toward professional enhancement and advancement.

## Step 6. Design a Faculty Reward Structure for Your Institution or State System

In order to sustain the participation of higher education faculty in your K–16 STEM initiative, there must be a mechanism for their work with K–12 teachers and their efforts to improve their own teaching to be part of the higher education faculty reward system. Success in this step is necessary to effect meaningful change in the culture of higher education. The following summary of action items is recommended.

When assembling the committee that leads development of a new higher education faculty reward system, it is important to enlist individuals with the authority and expertise to move your agenda forward. Early on, in the design phase, it is important to seek input from a broad spectrum of stake-holders at various levels in your college or university or from different higher education institutions in your state system.

It is important to adopt strategies that result in both top-down and bottom-up changes in the culture of your college or university or state higher education system. It is also important to recognize that culture change within each college or university does not have to be the same. Be flexible in designing your reward system; recognize that one size does not fit all even within a single institution.

It is helpful if you can build upon existing initiatives at the institutional, state, and national levels. Joining forces with those who can help you may increase your probability of achieving your goals.

Finally, it is important to engage significant numbers of faculty in the process of redesigning the higher education faculty reward system in ways that go beyond participation on the coordinating committee that is overseeing this strategy. For example, involving faculty in professional learning communities, bringing faculty together in statewide and local institute meetings or Academies for Learning, and operating a competitive small grants program can help build faculty "buy-in" for the desired changes.

## Step 7. Design a Comprehensive Evaluation System

Evaluation must be an essential component of your systemic K–16 STEM initiative. However, to optimize success it is necessary for the evaluation design to remain sufficiently flexible so that the plan can be changed to include different data-collection strategies or instruments that may be needed as the project evolves over multiple years.

It is important for the evaluation team to meet with project leaders in initial planning sessions for your K–16 STEM initiative. Evaluators can help project leaders to identify measurable goals and to set workable timelines for all strategies. Evaluators can identify areas of evaluation expertise needed to evaluate all goals. Based on these kinds of interactions with project staff, evaluators can create an evaluation team with necessary qualitative or quantitative expertise to cover all project sites and data collection for all strategies.

Just as it is important for your K–16 STEM leadership team to meet regularly, your evaluation team should also meet monthly and invite the project director (of your K–16 STEM initiative) to attend. It is important for the evaluation team to function as a truly collaborative team.

The evaluation team can also handle all of the Internal Research Board (IRB) requirements for your K–16 STEM initiative at all partner schools and colleges. The evaluation team can submit all evaluation instruments to appropriate IRB personnel for approval; ensure all evaluators are current in IRB protocol; and inform key university and school district administrators that IRB regulations are being followed to protect all project participants.

The evaluation team must also collaborate with your K–16 STEM leadership team. The evaluation team should share the evaluation plan and instruments with state and regional leaders early in the project; share formative and yearly evaluation reports with regional and state leaders; provide a formal mechanism for leaders to respond to evaluation reports; share raw data (except when promised confidentiality would be compromised) with partners who need them for local decision-making, professional presentations, or publications; and share evaluation findings with the national STEM community through professional presentations, articles, and books.

## Step 8. Sustaining Your STEM Initiative

Finally, it is important to attend to issues of sustainability and bringing your initiative to scale from the very beginning of your planning. As developed in chapter 9, it is important for your K–16 STEM leadership team to attend to issues of depth, sustainability, spread, and shift in ownership in order to succeed in bringing your STEM initiative to scale. It is likewise important for your K–16 STEM leadership team to deal head-on with challenges that may emerge related to trust, quality, and accountability. It is necessary for your K–16 STEM leadership team to answer the following questions if the initiative is to be sustained:

### Depth

- Do pre-service and in-service K–12 teachers have the sufficient science and mathematics content knowledge to bring students to high levels of achievement?
- How many higher education faculty participants are necessary in order to have the desired impact on K–12 teaching quality and on K–16 student achievement?

### Sustainability

- What are the competing demands and what are the consequential changes that must be continued and maintained over time?

*Spread*

- Are the changes institutionalized in school and college classrooms?

*Shift in Ownership*

- Is the initiative only being led from the top-down or has ownership moved to teachers, faculty, districts, schools, and universities?

*Trust*

- Has trust been built across K–12 and higher education cultures?

*Quality*

- How will you ensure your K–16 STEM initiative is characterized by quality?

*Accountability*

- Have you found ways to move beyond mere implementation and begin to examine, reflect, and transform K–16 STEM education?

## CONCLUSION

A first step toward the successful implementation of a systemic and sustainable K–16 STEM initiative is to believe that action must be taken. This book has argued for a K–16 approach to STEM improvement in the United States, one that involves both state and regional or local K–16 partnerships of teachers, faculty, educational administrators, and policy leaders. The authors hope that in these chapters your STEM leaders find sources of ideas, energy, and the commitment to stay the course. Our students in both schools and colleges and our country need for you to commit!

## NOTE

1. Sheila Jones is the project director in the Partnership for Reform In Science and Mathematics (PRISM), a systemic K–16 STEM initiative in Georgia. She

taught high school mathematics and is the senior executive director for P–16 Programs for the University System of Georgia. Janet S. Kettlewell is the principal investigator of PRISM. She is a teacher educator and the vice chancellor for P–16 Initiatives for the University System of Georgia. Ronald J. Henry is the co-principal investigator of PRISM. He is a physicist and the provost and senior vice president for Academic Affairs at Georgia State University in Atlanta.

# APPENDIX 2.1

PRISM Partnership Rubric

**Appendix 2.1.  PRISM Partnership Rubric**

| Indicators | Beginning | Emerging | Developing | Accomplished |
|---|---|---|---|---|
| Vision and Goals | Partners are together due to the nature of their work, but do not share a common vision and are concerned only with their own individual goals. | A shared vision emerges as partners work together, but the focus is still on individual goals. | Partners recognize the "value-added" of a shared vision and collaborate on some common goals. | Partners hold a shared vision and collaboratively develop and implement common goals. |
| Communication | The purpose of communication is to share individual needs. | Most communication focuses on sharing individual needs; however, some discussion takes place related to a shared vision and common goals. | Communication promotes progress toward achieving a shared vision and common goals. | Communication is both consistent and deliberate, and is seen as an important component of the success of the partnership. |
| Decision-Making | Most partners are represented by those with no authority to make changes; therefore, decisions are made apart from common goals. | Some partners are represented by those with limited authority to make small decisions that may contribute to common goals. | Most partners are represented by those with limited authority to make decisions that promote individual or organizational goals, but are less committed to making decisions toward common goals. | Partners with authority represent their organization to make collaborative decisions that meet common goals. |

| | | | | |
|---|---|---|---|---|
| Responsibility and Accountability | Partners are responsible and accountable for their own goals. One partner is in charge, and therefore, is accountable. | Some partners accept new roles of limited responsibility. Collaborative accountability is avoided, but an understanding of its importance is emerging. By common consent, one partner leads, and, therefore, is accountable. | Partners commit to new roles of shared responsibility as a result of a commitment to the common goals; but through an unspoken understanding or lack of communication, one partner emerges as accountable. | Partners hold themselves responsible and accountable for contributing to the common goals, as appropriate for the strengths of each partner (e.g., the level of commitment and specific contributions made by each organization). |
| Change and Sustainability | Partners recognize or even recommend that change is needed, but efforts are individual rather that collective and are not able to support change that is more than short-term. | Partners learn that all can contribute. They work together to identify necessary changes that meet individual and common goals. | Partners work to effect change that contributes to progress toward common goals. Some isolated changes remain in place for a certain amount of time; however, many are not yet sustainable. | Partners collaborate on common goals resulting in systemic change that is sustained beyond the grant. |

# APPENDIX 2.2

## PRISM Definition Document Example—Lead Teacher Roles and Responsibilities

Teacher leaders are in every school. The continuum of functions and tasks these individuals typically take on range from modeling good practice in the classroom to writing grants, to teaching professional development courses to serving on school and district committees. All of these are examples of teacher leadership.

The purpose of the selection of Lead Teachers for PRISM is to identify teachers who can lead within and beyond the classroom, influence others toward improved educational practice, and identify with and contribute to a community of teacher leaders.

### Characteristics:

- Recognized as a leader among fellow teachers and school administrators
- Communicates with various audiences (teachers, principal, system staff, parents, etc.)

### Leadership:

- Assists in the development of the school improvement plan
- Organizes and facilitates school-based science and mathematics study groups/learning communities

- Represents school and system at professional meetings and conferences
- Collaborates and networks with other PRISM Lead Teachers through the Teacher Advisory Council

## Professional Development:

- Participates in Lead Teacher Training
- Provides support to teachers on specific problems of practice by identifying and operationalizing appropriate professional development strategies
- Coordinates and facilitates teacher-managed professional development

## Communication:

- Initiates concise, timely, and accurate communication with school, district, and PRISM staff utilizing effective oral and written communication skills
- Shares professional development plans and reports with school, district, and PRISM staff
- Advocates for PRISM activities and strategies

## Evaluation:

- Assists in the evaluation of PRISM activities by maintaining and collecting activity documentation
- Serves as a contact between PRISM Evaluation team and PRISM teachers

# APPENDIX 6.1

Professional Learning Community Rubric

**Appendix 6.1.**

| Indicators | Beginning | Emerging | Developing | Accomplished |
|---|---|---|---|---|
| Shared Vision | The facilitator/leader of the learning community has a vision of teaching and learning which includes promoting intellectually challenging work for students and effective teaching practices. | A few of the members of the learning community share a vision of teaching and learning which promotes the development of intellectually challenging work for students and embodies the use of effective teaching practices. | Most of the members of the learning community share a vision of teaching and learning which promotes the development of intellectually challenging work for students and embodies the use of effective teaching practices. | All members of the learning community share a vision of teaching and learning which promotes the development of intellectually challenging work for students and embodies the use of effective teaching practices. |
| Shared Leadership | The learning community is organized and its work determined by someone perceived to be outside of the community and not directly related to the work. | The learning community is facilitated by one member who is responsible for organizing the meetings and work of the community. | The learning community is co-facilitated by a member from higher education and a member from K–12. | The learning community is facilitated through the input of all K–16 members equally sharing leadership responsibility. |
| K–16 Faculty Collaboration | The learning community is comprised of only K–12 faculty or higher education faculty, thus resulting in no K–16 collaboration. | The learning community is either school-based or university-based. Representatives from the other educational level may be invited to interact with the group from time to time resulting in tentative K–16 collaboration. | The learning community is either school-based or university-based, but includes a representative from the other educational level resulting in a limited K–16 collaboration. | The learning community is comprised of K–16 faculty due to the combined nature of their work, thus resulting in a substantial K–16 collaboration. |

| | | | |
|---|---|---|---|
| Collaborative Inquiry | Educators discuss the effectiveness of classroom practices and teaching materials currently used in their classrooms within their learning community. | Educators study and discuss research-based practices and how they relate to current practice within their learning community. | Educators discuss research-based practices within their learning community and individual members implement a practice in their classrooms based on need or interest. The member implementing decides how the effectiveness of the practice will be measured and reports results to the learning community. | Educators study research-based practices and collaboratively design an action research study that is conducted in their classrooms by the learning community and evidence of student achievement is documented. |
| Making Results Public | Learning community members share results of collaborative inquiry with their learning community. | Learning community members communicate results of their work with colleagues in their school and district. | Learning community members make presentations of results in regional, state, or national venues. | The results of the learning community work are published and accessible to a wide audience. |

# APPENDIX 6.2

## Definition of Professional Learning Community

Professional Learning Communities provide opportunities for K–16 educators to share what they know, consult with peers about problems of teaching and learning, and observe others at work. They promote a commitment to the following set of values which builds community and respect for diverse ideas:

- As their primary focus, the trying, testing, verifying, and replicating of teaching practices deemed to have a positive impact on student learning in science and mathematics in K–12 schools, colleges, and universities.
  - Practices that inform teaching in schools and colleges.
  - Practices that inform teacher preparation.
  - Practices that inform professional learning.
- A shared vision of teaching and learning among K–16 faculty participants.
  - A vision of high quality work for students that includes intellectually challenging tasks.
  - A vision than embodies effective practices, such as guided inquiry, cooperative learning, contextual teaching and learning, conceptual change, and problem-based learning.

- Collaboration between K–12 and higher education faculty.
  - They provide opportunities for K–16 educators to find solutions to vexing problems in the teaching and learning of science and mathematics.
  - They eliminate the isolation of faculty in the classroom.
- Shared leadership by faculty from schools, colleges, and universities—learning communities are faculty-led.
  - They provide opportunities for K–16 educators to reflect on practice and work with others to improve practice.
  - They are supported by the school, college, and university administration.
- Making the work of learning community participants public.
  - Learning community members share their work, making it open for discussion, verification, refutation, and modification.
  - Learning community members share effective and authenticated practices across schools, districts, regions, the state, and the nation.
- Results-oriented work.
  - That leads to improved student achievement.
  - That leads to improved teaching and learning of science and mathematics.
- Collaborative inquiry.
  - Reflect on and assess their teaching.
  - Explore and test new ideas, methods, and materials (implement a plan for improvement).
  - Assess effectiveness of plan for improvement (collect and analyze student achievement data and teacher effectiveness data).
  - Make decisions about which new approaches work and why.

# APPENDIX 7.1

PRISM Strategy #10

**Implementation Framework: Elements for Change**[1]

| Level | Policy | Practice |
|-------|--------|----------|
| USG | Advocacy policy | Models |
| | Teacher preparation policy | Chancellor's evaluation of presidents |
| | Strategic plan | Special funding initiatives |
| | | Strategic allocations |
| | | Showcase of faculty success |
| | | Showcase of scholarship of teaching |
| | | Structure to sustain: Advisory council |
| Institution | Advocacy policy | P and T results |
| | Mission | Financial incentives (e.g., small grants) |
| | Strategic plan | Showcase of faculty success |
| | Faculty handbook | Vice President for Academic Affairs as advocate |
| College | Mission and strategic plan include advocacy of work to improve own teaching and work with teacher preparation | P and T results |
| | | Salary increment results |
| | | Showcase of faculty success |
| | | Financial incentives |
| | P and T policy | Deans as advocates |
| | Workload policy | |
| | Salary policy | |
| | Post-tenure review policy | |
| Department | Advocacy work to improve teaching in higher education and K–12 | Work to improve teaching |
| | | P and T results |
| | P and T policy | Salary increment results |
| | Workload policy | Post-tenure review results |
| | Salary policy | Financial incentives |
| | Post-tenure review policy | Workload incentives |
| | | Chairs as advocates |

* "P and T" refers to "promotion and tenure."

## NOTE

1. Elements for Change should be considered a menu of options because not all apply at every higher education institution. All policy and practice strategies share the same goal: to improve student learning.

# APPENDIX 7.2

## Definitions, Examples of Evidence, and Illustrative Cases

## TEACHING

*Definition*: Scholarly teaching is teaching that focuses on student learning and is well grounded in the sources and resources appropriate to the field. The aim of scholarly teaching is to make transparent how faculty members have made learning possible (Shulman, 1998).

### Evidence of Scholarly Teaching:

- Evidence that the faculty member reads the pedagogical literature, or attends instructional development sessions, in his or her own discipline and then branches out to the broader pedagogical literature.
- Evidence that the faculty member tries some of the teaching methods from the literature/instructional development sessions in his or her own classes.
- Evidence that the faculty member assesses whether or not he/she has been successful in increasing student learning by doing some formative evaluation with his or her students, adjusting his or her approach, asking a peer to come into the class to review the changes he/she has implemented.

## Cases of Scholarly Teaching

*Case #1*: A mathematics faculty member read that time-on-task is a critical factor in student learning and, following formative evaluation, designed innovative web-based exercises to stimulate course-related student activity outside of class. Disciplinary colleagues at another university explored his course's Web site and, with the idea of possibly incorporating at least some features of the innovative course in their own courses, invited the mathematician to a seminar to explain the how and why of the innovations.

*Case #2*: A review of the pedagogical literature shows that teaching evolution effectively requires a simultaneous fostering of critical thinking, both within biology and about science in society. Evolution is the core of biology, and is central to public understanding and acceptance of basic science, but is rejected by a plurality of a public that accepts much pseudoscience. Data were gathered to determine whether student's initial acceptance of evolution affected their grades. In prior studies, initial rejection had been associated with lower grades. Several techniques were developed to reduce the conflict for such students without sacrificing the core science. Initial acceptance now has no relation to grades in the course.

## SCHOLARSHIP

### The Scholarship of Teaching and Learning

*Definition*: The Scholarship of Teaching and Learning is the "systematic examination of issues about student learning and instructional conditions that promote the learning (i.e., building on previous scholarship and shared concerns), that is subjected to blind review by peers who represent the judgment of the profession, and, after review, is disseminated to the professional community" (Research Universities Consortium for the Advancement of Scholarship of Teaching and Learning 2005).

### Evidence of the Scholarship of Teaching and Learning:

- Evidence that the faculty member's scholarship in the schools or in the university classroom is public, peer-reviewed, and critiqued.
- Evidence that the faculty member's scholarship is exchanged with other members of professional communities through postings on Web sites, presentations to his or her department or college, presentations at professional conferences, and/or written up and published.

- Evidence that the scholarship builds upon previous scholarship and shared concerns.
- Evidence that the scholarship contributes new questions and knowledge about teaching and learning.

## Cases of the Scholarship of Teaching and Learning (SoTL)

*Case #1*: This project addressed the problem that college-level required courses in introductory statistical analysis are generally unsuccessful in conveying the necessary concepts for students to apply or understand statistics. The project utilized digital video case studies of former students who took Statistical Techniques and who applied statistical tools in their workplace to solve significant problems. Each video addressed how the workplace problem originated and its characteristics, how statistical analysis was used to solve the problem, what the outcome was on the organization or environment, and the impact on the graduate's job or career. The problem definition component of the video was placed on a Web site and streamed to small groups of students outside of class, who analyzed the issue and proposed statistical methods for addressing the issue.

Each group's proposed solution was shared in class to stimulate discussion. A major component of the project was the development and application of assessment tools to determine if the digital video case studies were successful in meeting these goals. Another project element was the dissemination of the results of this SoTL research to the large community of scholars who teach such courses.

*Case #2*: Two chemistry faculty were awarded an NSF-ILI grant for the purchase of several Silicon Graphics (SGIs) in the winter of 2003 for use in undergraduate physical chemistry laboratories. These workstations allow for high-level molecular modeling simulations and the computation of various electronic and thermodynamic variables. Working with a third faculty member, whose specialty is the teaching of chemistry, the faculty determined that an evaluation of how the SGIs were incorporated into the curriculum and used by students would help improve the effectiveness of this technology as a teaching tool. The third faculty member observed the labs for two semesters, looking at types of student-student and student-faculty interactions. Students were also interviewed for thirty to fifty minutes each at three times during the year.

Based on the results of the observations and the interviews, the computational portion of the laboratory was revised. The three faculty, with the assistance of a student, have also created a Web site for general chemistry and given papers on their project at regional and national meetings.

*Case #3.* Two biology colleagues teach courses that follow one another in sequence. Students do not seem to be able to apply in one course what they learned in the previous one. Looking for ways to help students hone this skill, the biologists reviewed the literature on how students learn science, especially as it relates to the application of previously learned information to new situations. They decided to introduce the use of case studies into the courses, providing students opportunities to apply previously learned knowledge to new formats. At the end of the second semester, the faculty compared grades in the two courses (D, F, W grades) with grades from biology courses that did not use case studies. The work led to the development of a campus-wide workshop on the effective use of case studies to improve student learning (and retention), facilitated by the two biologists. The biologists subsequently submitted a paper to the *Journal of Biology Teaching* on their work.

## The Scholarship of Engagement

*Definition*: The Scholarship of Engagement in schools is characterized by the following: (1) it is to be conducted as an academic engagement with the public schools; (2) it is to involve the responsible application of knowledge, theory and/or conceptual framework to consequential problems; (3) it should test a research question or hypothesis; (4) one must be able to use the results to improve practice and inform further questions; and (5) resulting work should be available for dissemination for peer review of results (Glassick, Huber and Maeroff 1996).

## Evidence of the Scholarship of Engagement:

- Evidence that the faculty member designs and implements a research agenda in at least one area of need recognized by the public schools.
- Evidence that the faculty member applies relevant knowledge toward resolution of the identified need.
- Evidence that the faculty member assesses the impact of the engagement.
- Evidence that the faculty member disseminates for peer review the results of the outreach.

## Cases of the Scholarship of Engagement

*Case #1*: Faculty and students in Colleges of Arts and Sciences collaborated with faculty and students of local high schools in a structured, discipline-based learning community to improve the quality of teaching and learning of the discipline. Through a service-learning course, students who were mentored by college faculty worked with teachers to design and implement lessons with up-to-date content, constructivist teaching strategies, and learning outcomes appropriate to the grade level of the students. The research question was: To what extent does the placement of mentored undergraduate majors and graduate students in high school classrooms, working as partners to teachers, improve the quality of teaching and learning science and mathematics?

Findings of each classroom were analyzed and applied to enhance the feasibility and quality of the learning community, and to increase the likelihood of replication and sustainability. Results of this learning community were shared statewide and nationally. With the leadership of college faculty, papers were co-authored by members in the learning community and published in peer-reviewed journals.

*Case #2*: Higher Education faculty contributed to the scholarship of engagement by applying their knowledge and expertise within a collaboration to improve teaching and learning in a K–12 course. The research question was: What are the results of a K–12 and higher education faculty collaborative that is designed to assess areas for improvement, develop strategies, and team-teach a K–12 course? A team of K–12 and higher education faculty worked together to assess and redesign a course. Strategies and course changes were based upon study of curricula, classroom observations, and student data.

The weakest areas of student learning as indicated by these data were the points of focus for analysis, study of related literature, and development of effective classroom strategies. The experimental course was team-taught collaboratively integrating content knowledge, pedagogical knowledge, and teacher practice knowledge into the delivery. The team collected and analyzed data to measure increased student learning. Data were fine enough to identify those strategies that worked and those that need refinement. This information was used to further improve and redeliver the course. The re-designed course and the procedure for course development and improvement were presented at regional conferences. Course and delivery format were adopted by district administrations.

## The Scholarship of Discovery

*Definition*: The Scholarship of Discovery is basic research in the disciplines including the creative work of faculty in the literary, visual, and performing arts. It is the "pursuit of knowledge for its own sake, a fierce determination to give free rein to fair and honest inquiry, wherever it may lead" (Glassick, Huber, and Maeroff 1996). It contributes to the stock of human knowledge in the academic disciplines.

**Evidence of the Scholarship of Discovery:**

- Evidence that the faculty member's research is innovative (as opposed to routine) as judged by peers at the institution and elsewhere.
- Evidence that the faculty member's research represents quality, rather than mere quantity.
- Evidence of the faculty member's publications in high-quality refereed journals and the quality and quantity of citations and reprints of his or her research publications. If appropriate for the discipline, evidence of the ability to attract extramural funding.
- Evidence of invited seminars and presentations (abstracts), if travel funds are provided, are also an indication of the Scholarship of Discovery.

**Cases of the Scholarship of Discovery**

*Case #1*: This project was motivated by a perceived application of algebraic group theory to solving large classes of differential equations. Historically, engineers and others needing to solve differential equations in their work must rely upon approximation methods as most differential equations are considered unsolvable. Hence, the project had the potential not only to contribute to the base of knowledge in the field, but also to aid those who use mathematics in their field. The investigator undertook study to become more knowledgeable about the area of differential equations.

An initial hypothesis was investigated through support from an internal research grant. It was discovered that finite algebraic groups are connected to differential equations having a very specific type of solution. The results of the work were presented at a subsequent conference and published in a refereed journal. They have since been used in proving consequential results in a new and growing field of mathematics and in the development of software used to solve differential equations.

*Case #2*: A research project dealing with the hydrology of a region was formulated when the researcher learned of the presence of springs during an agricultural workshop. None of the springs had ever been described or their waters analyzed, so the project had the potential for bringing substantial revision to the hydrology of the region. A small development grant was awarded for the purchase of analytical equipment. Students were engaged to periodically conduct carefully controlled assays of water chemistry and quality. Following two years of data-gathering, a report was submitted to and was accepted by the State Geologic Survey as a water supply bulletin. The collaborative work with students was described and accepted for publication in a peer-reviewed journal on science teaching.

## SERVICE

*Definition*: Service is outreach or engagement by higher education faculty for the purpose of contributing to the public good. Contributions to the public good may include faculty work that contributes to solutions to complex societal problems, to the quality of life of Georgia's citizens, and to the advancement of public higher education. In the case of service to the public schools, the intent should be for the improvement of teaching quality and student learning. The following activities might be included in work with the schools: involvement in learning communities, workshops given based on need, collaborative development of courses, unit-writing for the new Georgia Performance Standards, design of field experiences to support existing courses, engagement in co-observation/vertical alignment, etc.

### Evidence of Service:

- Evidence that the faculty member links his or her work in some way to public contemporary issues and/or to improving the quality of life.
- Evidence that the faculty member, through his or her scholarly work and/or service, applies his or her knowledge toward solutions to complex societal problems and human needs.
- Evidence that the faculty member contributes to the continuous improvement of public higher education.
- Evidence that the faculty member contributes in some way to the public good.

### Cases of Service to the Schools

*Case #1*: A professor of mathematics collaborated with high school teachers to construct effective learning modules, inclusive of a focal problem, content, design, implementation, and assessment, related to the topical expertise of the faculty. The development of each module was based on the needs specific to a grade level and classroom, including the resource base of the classroom, level of interest and competency of the teacher, and level of competency and required knowledge of the students. The professor prepared the module and guided the teacher in its implementation. In turn, the teacher and students provided feedback on the feasibility and compatibility of the module to each classroom culture.

*Case #2*: Higher Education faculty regularly engaged in group discussions via a professional learning community with K–12 faculty. These groups studied student data, reviewed literature on best practices, and shared experiences with teaching and learning. One of the main accomplishments was collaborative planning of customized professional learning for teachers. The learning community also provided a forum for ongoing discussion about classroom implementation of the professional learning.

*Case #3*: Higher education faculty and high school physics and physical science teachers met to discuss and develop seamless alignment of the curricula. Student content knowledge, study skills, and conceptual understanding were all discussed. High school and higher education faculty observed each other teaching similar or aligned topics for the purpose and applied lessons learned to the development of better-aligned curriculum.

# REFERENCES

ACT. 2006. *Developing the Education Pipeline*. Iowa City, IA: ACT.

American Association for the Advancement of Science. 1993. *Benchmarks for Science Literacy*. New York: Oxford University Press.

American Diploma Project Network. 2005. Launched by Achieve, Inc. http://www.achieve.org/

Angelo, T. A., and K. P. Cross. 1993. *Classroom Assessment Techniques: A Handbook for College Teachers*. San Francisco, CA: Jossey-Bass.

Black, P., and D. Wiliam. 1998. "Inside the Black Box: Raising Standards through Classroom Assessment." *Phi Delta Kappan*, 80(2), 139–148.

Bransford, J. D., A. L. Brown, and R. Cocking, eds. 1999. *How People Learn: Brain, Mind, Experience, and School*. Washington, DC: National Academy Press.

Board of Regents of the University System of Georgia. 1998. *Regents' Principles for the Preparation of Teachers for the Schools*. Atlanta. www.usg.edu/academics/initiatives/teachprep/principles.phtml.

Business-Higher Education Forum. 2005. "Commitment to America's Future: Responding to the Crisis in Mathematics and Science." Washington, DC. www.bhef.com/publications/MathEduReport-press.pdf.

Business-Higher Education Forum. 2006. "Tapping America's Potential: The Education for Innovation Initiative." Washington, DC.

Business Roundtable. 2005. "Tapping America's Potential: The Education for Innovation Initiative." Washington, DC.

Callow-Heuser, C. A., R. T. Torres, and H. J. Chapman. 2005. *Evidence: An Essential Tool: Planning for and Gathering Evidence Using the Design-Implementation-Outcomes (DIO): Cycle of Evidence*. NSF Document Number NSF0531. Logan,

UT: Consortium for Building Evaluation Capacity, Utah State University. Accessed May 29, 2007, from http://www.nsf.gov/pubs/2005/nsf0531/nsf0531.pdf.

Cerbin, B., and Kopp, B. 2008. "A Brief Introduction to College Lesson Study." Accessed January 15, 2008, from www.uwlax.edu/sotl/lsp/index2.htm.

Chatterji, M. 2004. "Evidence on 'What Works': An Argument for Extended-Term Mixed-Method (ETMM) Evaluation Designs." *Educational Researcher*, 33(9), 3–13.

Coburn, C. E. 2003. Rethinking Scale: Moving Beyond Numbers to Deep and Lasting Change. *Educational Researcher*, 32(6), 3–12.

Cohen, D. K., and Hill, H. C. 1998. "State Policy and Classroom Performance: Mathematics Reform in California." *CPRE Policy Briefs* (RB-23-January, 1–14). Philadelphia: Consortium for Policy Research in Education, Graduate School of Education, University of Pennsylvania.

College Board. 2007. Accessed July 9, 2008, from http://professionals.collegeboard.com/profdownload/Integrated_Math_Standards.pdf.

Committee on Prospering in the Global Economy of the 21st Century. 2007. *Rising Above the Gathering Storm: Energizing and Employing America for a Brighter Economic Future*. Washington, DC: National Academy Press.

Covey, S. R. 1989. *The Seven Habits of Highly Effective People*. New York: Free Press.

Cox, M., and Richlin, L., eds. 2004. *New Directions for Teaching and Learning*, no. 97. San Francisco: Jossey-Bass.

Darling-Hammond, L. 2000. "Teacher Quality and Student Achievement: A Review of State Policy Evidence." *Education Policy Analysis Archives*, 8(1). Accessed June 27, 2008, from http://epaa.asu.edu/epaa/v8n1/.

Darling-Hammond, L., and L. Post. 2000. "Inequality in Teaching and Schools." In *A Nation at Risk: Preserving Public Education as an Engine for Social Mobility*, ed. R. D. Kahlenberg. New York: Century Foundation Press.

Darling-Hammond, L., A. E. Wise, and S. R. Pease. 1983. "Teacher Evaluation in the Organizational Context: A Review of the Literature." *Review of Educational Research*, 53, 285–237.

Davis, E. 2007. "Chancellor Erroll B. Davis Endorses the State Board of Education's Adoption of the New High School Graduation Rule." Georgia Department of Education, October, 19, 2007. http://www.doe.k12.ga.us/math.aspx.

Dewey, J. 1993. *How We Think: A Restatement of the Relation of Reflective Thinking to the Educative Process*, revised ed. Boston: DC Heath.

Douglass, J. 2006. "The Waning of America's Higher Education Advantage: International Competitors Are No Longer Number Two and Have Big Plans in the Global Economy." UC Berkeley: Center for Studies in Higher Education.

DuFour, R., and R. Eaker. 1998. *Professional Learning Communities at Work: Best Practices for Enhancing Student Achievement*. Bloomington, IN: Solution Tree.

Education Trust. 2000. Accessed December 16, 2002, from http://www.edtrust.org.

Ellett, C. D., and J.A. Monsaas. 2007. "Summary of the Development and Use of the Inventory for Teaching and Learning (ITAL) in the External Evaluation of the Georgia Partnership for Reform in Science and Mathematics (PRISM)." Accessed September 5, 2007, from http://hub.mspnet.org/index.cfm/14286.

Frechtling, J. 2002. *The 2002 User-Friendly Handbook for Project Evaluation.* Division of Research Evaluation and Communication. (Washington, DC: The National Science Foundation.

Friedman, T. L. 2005. *The World is Flat: A Brief History of the Twenty-First Century.* New York: Farrar, Straus, and Giroux.

Gardner, P. L. 1998. "The Development of Males' and Females' Interests in Science and Technology" in *Interest and Learning: Proceedings of the Seeon Conference on Interest and Gender,* eds. L. Hoffmann, A. Krapp., K. A. Renninger and J. Baumert. Kiel, Germany: IPN, 1998, 41–57.

Gardner, P. L., and P. Tamir. 1989. "Interest in Biology. Part I: A Multidimensional Construct." *Journal of Research in Science Teaching,* 26(5), 409–423.

Gilbert, L., M. Hughes, and K. Miller. 2008. "P–5 Math Endorsement: Impacts and Lessons Learned." Presentation at the 2008 Math and Science Partnership (MSP) Learning Network Conference, Washington, DC.

Gips, C. J. 1998. "The Public Schools Rewards Project: A Higher Ed Tough One." In *Making a Place in the Faculty Rewards System for Work with K–12,* eds. C. Gips and C. Stoel. Washington, DC: American Association for Higher Education, 5–32.

Gladwell, M. 2000. *The Tipping Point: How Little Things Can Make a Big Difference.* New York: Little, Brown and Company.

Glassick, C. E., M. T. Huber, and G. I. Maeroff. 1996. *Scholarship Assessed: Evaluation of the Professoriate.* San Francisco: Jossey-Bass Publishers.

Gomez, M., J. Bissell, L. Danziger, and R. Casselman. 1990. *To Advance Learning: A Handbook on Developing K–12 Postsecondary Partnerships.* Lanham, MD: University Press of America.

Good, T. L. 1983. "Recent Classroom Research: Implications for Teacher Education" In *Essential Knowledge for Beginning Educators,* ed. D. C. Smith. Washington, DC: American Association of Colleges for Teacher Education.

Good, T. L., and J. E. Brophy. 1986. *Educational Psychology, 3rd Edition.* New York: Longman.

Guskey, T. R. 2000. *Evaluating Professional Development.* Thousand Oaks: Corwin Press.

Hahs-Vaughn, D. L., and A. J. Onwuegbuzie. 2006. "Estimating and Using Propensity Score Analysis with Complex Samples." *Journal of Experimental Education,* 75(1), 31–65.

Henderson, A. T., and K. L. Mapp. 2002. *A New Wave of Evidence: The Impact of School, Family, and Community Connections on Student Achievement.* Austin, TX: Southwest Educational Development Laboratory, National Center for Family and Community Connections with Schools.

Henry, R. J., and J. S. Kettlewell, J. S. 1999. "Georgia's P–16 Partnership." *Metropolitan Universities, 10*, 33–40.

Hewson, P. W., and N. R. Thorley. 1989. "The Conditions of Conceptual Change in the Classroom." *International Journal of Science Education, 11*(5), 541–553.

Hidi, S., and K. A. Renninger. 2006. "The Four-Phase Model of Interest Development." *Educational Psychologist 41*(2), 111–127.

Holt, D. B. 2002. *Got Milk? Marketing Milk as a Commodity.* New York: University of Oxford Advertising Educational Foundation.

Hord, S. M. 1997. "Professional Learning Communities: What Are They and Why Are They Important?" *Issues...about Change, 6*(1), 1–8.

Hotchkiss, J. L., R. E. Moore, and M. M. Pitts. 2006. "Freshman Learning Communities, College Performance, and Retention." *Education Economics 14*(2), 197–210.

Huba, M. E., and J. E. Freed.1999. *Learner-Centered Assessment on College Campuses: Shifting the Focus from Teaching to Learning.* Needham Heights, MA: Allyn and Bacon.

Huffman, J. B., and K. A. Hipp. 2000. "Creating communities of Learners: The Interaction of Shared Leadership, Shared Vision, and Supportive Conditions." Paper presented at the Annual Meeting of the American Educational Research Association. New Orleans, LA, April 24–28.

Japan Ministry of Education, Science, and Culture. 1989. "1989 Japanese National Course of Study." Translated by the Japan Society of Mathematical Education.

Johnson, R. B., and A. J. Onwuegbuzie. 2004. "Mixed Methods Research: A Research Paradigm Whose Time Has Come." *Educational Researcher, 33*(7), 14–26.

Joyce, B., and B. Showers. 2002. *Student Achievement Through Staff Development,* 3rd ed. Alexandria, VA: Association for Supervision and Curriculum Development.

Karabenick, S., and M. Maehr. 2008. MSP-MAP Final Report. Accessed June 25, 2008, from http://ma.mspnet.org/index.cfm/15221.

Kettlewell, J. S., J. Kaste, and S. Jones. 2000. "The Georgia Story of P–16 Partnerships." 1999 Yearbook of the Politics of Education Association.

Kilpatrick, J., J. Swafford, and B. Findell, eds. 2001. *Adding It Up: Helping Children Learn Mathematics.* Washington, DC: National Academy Press.

King, J. A. 2007. "Developing Evaluation Capacity Through Process Use." *New Directions in Evaluation 116*, 45–59.

Kingsley, G., and M. R. Waschak. 2005. "Finding Value and Meaning in the Concept of Partnership." Paper presented at the MSP Evaluation Summit: Evidence-Based Findings from MSPs, September 2005, Minneapolis, MN. Accessed December 5, 2007, from http://hub.mspnet.org/index.cfm/13778.

Kozaitis, K. A. 2008. "Educational Reform in Science and Mathematics: An Anthropological Perspective." *Practicing Anthropology, 30*(2), 14–18.

Kujawa, S., and L. Huske. 1995. *Strategic Teaching and Reading Project Guidebook.* Oak Brook, IL: North Central Regional Educational Laboratory.

Kutal, C., F. Butler, S. Connor, C. Ellett, R. J. Henry, S. Hessinger, J. Kettlewell, K. Kozaitis, H. R. Miller, F. Rich, N. Vandergrift, and D. Zinsmeister. 2006. "Developing a Reward Structure for Higher Education Faculty Involvement in K–12 Schools." National Science Foundation MSPnet. http://hub.mspnet.org/media/data/Kutal_et_al.pdf?media_000000002245.pdf.

Leo, T., and D. E. Cowan. 2000."Launching Professional Learning Communities: Beginning Actions." *Issues...about Change*, 8(1), 1–16.

Lewis, C. 2002. *Lesson Study: A Handbook of Teacher-Led Instructional Change.* Philadelphia: Research for Better Schools.

Loucks-Horsley, S., N. Love, K. Stiles, S. Mundry, and P. Hewson. 2003. *Designing Professional Development for Teachers of Science and Mathematics.* Thousand Oaks, CA: Corwin Press.

Love, N. 2002. *Using Data/Getting Results: A Practical Guide for School Improvement in Mathematics and Science.* Norwood, MA: Christopher-Gordon Publishers, Inc.

Ma, L. 1999. *Knowing and Teaching Elementary Mathematics.* Mahwah, NJ: Lawrence Erlbaum.

Maguire Associates, Inc. 2005. "Framing a PRISM Public Awareness Campaign: A Market Research Report." Bedford, MA.

Maguire Associates, Inc. 2007. "Preliminary Evaluation of the Public Awareness Campaign: A Market Research Report." Concord, MA.

Massy, W. F., S. W. Graham, and P. M. Short. 2007. *Academic Quality Work: A Handbook for Improvement.* San Francisco: Jossey-Bass.

MindPower, Inc. 2005. "First Look at a Public Awareness Campaign for PRISM." Atlanta, GA.

Mosteller, F., B. Nave, and E. J. Miech. 2004. "Why We Need a Structured Abstract in Education Research." *Educational Researcher, Jan/Feb,* 29–34.

Murphey, C. U., and D. W. Lick. 2005. *Whole Faculty Study Groups: Creating Professional Learning Communities that Target Student Learning,* 3rd ed. Thousand Oaks, California: Corwin Press.

National Academy for K–12 Science and Mathematics Education Leadership. 1997. http://www.wested.org/cs/we/view/serv/55.

National Academy of Sciences. 2007. *Rising above the Gathering Storm: Energizing and Employing America for a Brighter Economic Future* Washington, DC: National Academy Press.

National Association of State Directors of Career Technical Education Consortium. 2006. Sample Plans of Study. www.careerclusters.org/plans.htm.

National Center for Education Statistics. 2004. "Trends in International Mathematics and Science Study (TIMSS) 2003." Washington, DC.

National Council of Teachers of Mathematics. 1989. *Curriculum and Evaluation Standards for School Mathematics.* Reston, VA: National Council of Teachers of Mathematics.

National Research Council. 1989. *Everybody Counts: A Report to the Nation on the Future of Mathematics Education.* Washington, DC: National Academy Press.

National Research Council. 1996. *National Science Education Standards*. Washington, DC: National Academy Press.

National Research Council. 1999. *Transforming Undergraduate Education in Science, Mathematics, Engineering, and Technology*. Washington, DC: National Academy Press.

National Science Foundation Math and Science Program. 2002. Accessed June 20, 2008, from http://www.nsf.gov/ehr/MSP/.

National Staff Development Council. 2001. *Standards for Staff Development*. Oxford, OH.

Ngari, M. H., L. Hansche Despriet, and J. Monsaas. 2008. "The Effectiveness of a Summer Program to Attract Minority Students into Mathematics and Science Teaching, their Attitudes towards Science, Mathematics and Teaching, and their Decision to Attend College." Paper Presented at the Annual Meeting of the American Educational Research Association, New York, March.

North Carolina Math Standards. 2003. Accessed July 9, 2008, from http://www.ncpublicschools.org/curriculum/mathematics/scos/2003/k-8/index.

Patton, M. Q. 2002. *Qualitative Research and Evaluation Methods*, 3rd ed. Thousand Oaks, CA: Sage Publications.

Pelligrino, J. W., N. Chudowsky, and R. Glaser, eds. 2001. *Knowing What Students Know: The Science and Design of Educational Assessment*. Washington, DC: National Academy Press.

Phi Delta Kappa International. 2002. "An External Audit of the Georgia Quality Core Curriculum." January 24.

Preskill, H. 2008. "Evaluation's Second Act: A Spotlight on Learning." *American Journal of Evaluation*, 29(2), 127–138.

Project Kaleidoscope. 2006. "Transforming America's Scientific and Technological Infrastructure. Recommendations for Urgent Action." *Report on Reports II*. Washington, DC. www.pkal.org/documents/ReportOnReportsII.cfm. Accessed June 20, 2008.

Public Agenda. 2006. "Reality Check: Are Parents and Students Ready for More Math and Science?" New York.

Public Agenda. 2007. "Important, but Not for Me: Parents and Students in Kansas and Missouri Talk About Math, Science, and Technology Education." New York.

Research Universities Consortium for the Advancement of the Scholarship of Teaching and Learning. 2005. *Policies and Procedures Supporting the Scholarship of Teaching and Learning in the Research University, Draft*. Stanford, CA: Carnegie Consortium for the Advancement of the Scholarship of Teaching and Learning.

Rich, F., C. Chance, and D. Battles. 2007. "Effecting Institutional Change in Faculty Roles, Rewards, and Recognition—A Case Study from Georgia Southern University." *Widening Participation and Lifelong Learning*, 9(3), 47–50.

Rivkin, S., E. Hanushek, and J. Kain. 1998. "Teachers, Schools, and Academic Achievement." National Bureau of Economic Research, Working Paper no. 6691.

Rosebery, A. S., B. Warren, and F. R. Conant. 1992. "Appropriating Scientific Discourse: Findings from Language Minority Classrooms." *The Journal of Learning Sciences*, 2(1), 61–94.

Rosenbaum, P. R., and D. B. Rubin. 1983. "The Central Role of the Propensity Score in Observational Studies for Causal Effects." *Biometrika*, 70(1), 41–55.

Rosenshine, B., and N. F. Furst. 1973. "The Use of Direct Observation to Study Teaching," in *Handbook of Research on Teaching* (2nd Ed), ed. R. M. W. Travers. Chicago: Rand McNally.

Ross, J. A., D. McDougall, A. Hogaboam-Gray, and A. LeSage. 2003. "A Survey Measuring Elementary Teachers' Implementation of Standards-Based Mathematics Teaching." *Journal for Research in Mathematics Education*, 34(4), 344–454.

Rossi, P. H., M. W. Lipsey, and H.E. Freeman. 2003. *Evaluation: A Systemic Approach*, 7th ed. Thousand Oaks, CA: Sage Publications.

Sanders, J. R., ed. 1994. *The Program Evaluation Standards: How to Assess Evaluations of Educational Programs*, 2nd ed. Thousand Oaks, CA: Sage Publications.

Sanders, W., and Rivers, J. 1996. *Cumulative and Residual Effects of Teachers on Future Academic Achievement*. Knoxville, TN: University of Tennessee Value-Added Research and Assessment Center.

Sawada, D., M. Piburn, K. Falconer, J. Turley, R. Benford, and I. Bloom. 2000. *Reformed Teaching Observation Protocol (RTOP) Training Guide*. ACEPT Technical Reports N0.1NOO-1. Tempe, AZ: Arizona Collaborative for Excellence in the Preparation of Teachers.

Scherer, J. 2006. *Partnership Implementation in the MSP Program. NSF Document Number 02516*. COSMOS Corporation: Math and Science Partnership Program Evaluation (MSP-PE). Accessed December 7, 2007, from http://hub.mspnet.org/media/data/Partnerships.pdf?media_000000002516.pdf, 10–58.

Schneider, B., C. B. Swanson, and C. Riegle-Crumb. 1997. "Opportunities for Learning: Course Sequences and Positional Advantages." *School Psychology of Education*, 2(1), 25–53.

Schmoker, M. 2002. "Up and Away. The Formula is Well Known, Now we Need to Follow It." *Journal of Staff Development*, 23(2), 10–13.

Shulman, L. 1999. "Course Anatomy: The Dissection and Analysis of Knowledge Through Teaching" in *The Course Portfolio: How Faculty Can Examine Their Teaching to Advance Practice and Improve Student Learning*, ed. P. Hutchings. Washington, DC: American Association for Higher Education, 5–12.

Senge, P., N. Cambron-McCabe, T. Lucas, B. Smith, J. Dutton, and A. Kleiner. 2000. *Schools that Learn: A Fifth Discipline Fieldbook*. New York: Doubleday.

Shadish, W. R., T. D. Cook, and D. T. Campbell. 2002. *Experimental and Quasi-Experimental Design for Generalized Causal Inference*. Boston: Houghton Mifflin.

Sparks, D. 2002. *Designing Powerful Professional Development for Teachers and Principals*. Oxford, OH: National Staff Development Council.

Steen, L. A. 1999. "Algebra for All in Eighth Grade. What's the Rush?" *Middle Matters*, 8(1), 6–7.

Steinberg, L. 1996. *Beyond the Classroom: Why School Reform Has Failed and What Parents Need to Do*. New York, NY: Simon and Schuster.

Thomas B. Fordham Institute. 2000. *State of the State Standards, 2000, Georgia*. www.fordhamfoundation.org.

Thomas B. Fordham Institute. 2005. *State of the State Standards, 2005, Georgia.* http://www.edexcellence.net.

Title II of NCLB. 2002. Accessed June 20, 2008, from http://www.ed.gov/programs/teacherqual/index.html.

U.S. Department of Education. 2000. Office of Vocational Technical Education, Career Cluster Brochure.

Wandersee, J. H., J. J. Mintzes, and J. D. Novak. 1994. "Research on Alternative Conceptions in Science." In *Handbook of Research on Science Teaching and Learning,* ed. D.L. Gabel. New York: Macmillan, 177–210.

Wellman, B., and L. Lipton. 2004. *Data-Driven Dialogue: A Facilitator's Guide to Collaborative Inquiry.* (Sherman, CT: MiraVia.

Wenger, E., R. McDermott, and W. Snyder. 2002. *Cultivating Communities of Practice: A Guide to Managing Knowledge.* Cambridge, MA: Harvard Business School Press.

Wheatley, M. J. 2002. *Turning to One Another: Simple Conversations to Restore Hope to the Future.* San Francisco: Berrett-Koehler Publishers.

Wiggins, G., and J. McTighe. 2005. *Understanding by Design.* 2nd ed. Alexandria, VA: ASCD.

Wilson, S. M., R. E. Floden, and J. Ferrini-Mundy. 2001. *Teacher Preparation Research: Current Knowledge, Gaps and Recommendations.* Seattle: Center for the Study of Teaching and Policy.

Winkler, A., and J. Fretchling. 2005. *MSP Evaluation Summit: Focus Partnership. Evaluating New versus Mature Partnerships: How Evaluation Questions May Change Based on Partnership Longevity.* FOCUS MSP, Westat: Unpublished working paper. http://hub.mspnet.org/media/data/Winkler_Frechtling.pdf?media_000000002060.pdf.

Wolff, T. 2001. "A Practitioner's Guide to Successful Coalitions," *American Journal of Community Psychology,* 29(2), 173–191.

Worthen, B. R., J. R. Sanders, and J. L. Fitzpatrick. 2003. *Program Evaluation: Alternative Approaches and Practical Guidelines,* 3rd ed. Needham Heights, MA: Allyn and Bacon.

Wubbels, T., M. Brekelmans, and H. Hooymayers. 1992. "Do Teacher Ideals Distort the Self-Reports of Their Interpersonal Behavior?" *Teaching and Teacher Education,* 8, 47–58.

Zemsky, R. 2008. "Understanding the Limits to Reform" *The Chronicle of Higher Education.* Accessed January 11, 2008, from http://chronicle.com/review/brainstorm/article/?id=111.

Zhang, X., J. McInerney, J. Frechtling, G. Nyre, J. Michie, A. Miyaoka, J. Wells, and H. M. Arista. 2007. "Effect of STEM Faculty Engagement in MSP: A Longitudinal Perspective." National Science Foundation MSPnet. hub.mspnet.org/media/data/MSP_STEM_Year_3_Report.pdf?media_000000002457.pdf.

# ABOUT THE CONTRIBUTORS

**Dava C. Coleman** is a regional director in the Partnership for Reform in Science and Mathematics (PRISM), a systemic K–16 STEM initiative in Georgia. She is a high school teacher with Jackson County Schools in Jefferson, Georgia.

**Rosalind Barnes Fowler** is the public awareness director in the Partnership for Reform in Science and Mathematics (PRISM), a systemic K–16 STEM initiative in Georgia. She is a project director and communications professional in the P–16 department for the University System of Georgia.

**Ronald J. Henry** is the co-principal investigator in the Partnership for Reform in Science and Mathematics (PRISM), a systemic K-16 STEM initiative in Georgia. He is a physicist and the provost and senior vice president for Academic Affairs at Georgia State University in Atlanta.

**Sabrina A. Hessinger** is a regional co-principal investigator in the Partnership for Reform in Science and Mathematics (PRISM), a systemic K–16 STEM initiative in Georgia. She is an associate professor of mathematics and special assistant to the dean of the College of Science and Technology in charge of the STEM Initiative at Armstrong Atlantic State University in Savannah.

**Sheila Jones** is the project director in the Partnership for Reform in Science and Mathematics (PRISM), a systemic K–16 STEM initiative in Georgia. She taught high school mathematics and is the senior executive director for P–16 Programs for the University System of Georgia.

**Janet S. Kettlewell** is the principal investigator of the Partnership for Reform in Science and Mathematics (PRISM), a systemic K–16 STEM initiative in Georgia. She is a teacher educator and the vice chancellor for P–16 Initiatives for the University System of Georgia.

**Charles Kutal** is a regional co-principal investigator in the Partnership for Reform in Science and Mathematics (PRISM), a systemic K-16 STEM initiative in Georgia. He is a professor of chemistry and associate dean of the College of Arts and Sciences at the University of Georgia.

**Amy S. Mast** is the associate director for K–12 in the Partnership for Reform in Science and Mathematics (PRISM), a systemic K–16 STEM initiative in Georgia. She is an education policy specialist and the director of implementation for Georgia's Alliance of Education Agency Heads.

**Mary Jo McGee-Brown** is the lead external qualitative evaluator of PRISM. She is the president of Qualitative Research & Evaluation for Action, Inc. and formerly taught qualitative research and data analysis at the University of Georgia.

**H. Richard Miller** is a regional co-principal investigator in PRISM. He is an astrophysicist and chair of the Department of Physics and Astronomy at Georgia State University in Atlanta.

**Judith A. Monsaas** is the lead evaluator of the Partnership for Reform in Science and Mathematics (PRISM), a systemic K–16 STEM initiative in Georgia. She is a professor of education specializing in evaluation, assessment, statistics and research and is the executive director for P–16 evaluation and assessment for the University System of Georgia.

**Fred Rich** is a regional co-principal Investigator in PRISM. He is a professor of geology at Georgia Southern University. He is a palynologist and paleoecologist by training, but has had a long interest in earth science education for teachers. He is currently affiliated with the St. Catherines Island (Ga) Sea Turtle Conservation Program.

**Nancy Vandergrift** is a regional program coordinator in the Partnership for Reform in Science and Mathematics (PRISM), a systemic K–16 STEM initiative in Georgia. She is also a program coordinator for the College of Education at the University of Georgia.